Born of a Woman

Woman's Place in the Scheme of Redemption

Dene Ward

DeWard™
for your journey

Born of a Woman: Woman's Place in the Scheme of Redemption
© 2018 by DeWard Publishing Company, Ltd.
P.O. Box 6259, Chillicothe, Ohio 45601
800.300.9778
www.deward.com

Cover design by Barry Wallace.

Printed in the United States of America.

ISBN: 978-1-936341-99-3

TABLE OF CONTENTS

Mothers and Daughters

The Women in Jesus' Ministry

The Worthy Woman

Comprehensive Reviews

EXPLANATION OF THE LESSONS

These lessons are designed to show God's plan of salvation through the women of the Bible, and to apply specific principles from each lesson to our lives so that we may "grow up in all things into Him. ..." By doing this women will see that there is much for them to do for the Lord within the limitations He has set.

Each lesson uses a different combination of the following features:

1. Objective questions: Short answer, multiple choice, matching, true/false, etc., to make certain the text has been studied and understood. The true/false and multiple choice are decidedly tricky and ambiguous. More than one correct answer may be given depending upon the way it is read. Do not get hung up on there being one correct answer. A person is correct so long as their thinking is correct.

2. Research questions: To gain facility with concordances, Bible dictionaries, atlases etc., not as a source of Truth, but as an enhancement to our knowledge and understanding.

3. Discussion questions: To find applicable passages elsewhere, to speculate a little (always remembering that it is speculation), and to get down to the "nitty-gritty" of applying particulars to our lives. Students are encouraged to keep a notebook specifically for answering these questions, as it was not possible to allow enough room in a book of this size.

4. The purpose of the woman studied: What did she do to further God's plan? (Bear children in the line of Christ, save Israel from destruction, spread the Word etc.) Sometimes a woman's purpose is not revealed (but not often) and sometimes she did not fulfill her purpose so God used her actions in some other way to further His plan.

5. The example the woman set: What did she do that we should or should not imitate?

6. Text: The verses from which the lesson is taken. These are primarily for the objective questions. The discussion questions may require extra research.

There are three types of lessons:

1. Individual women: These contain the most material and require the most down-to-earth applications.

2. Groups of women: These women all have something in common, and the application is more general.

3. Surveys on a class of woman: The application here may be doctrinal: queens—our relationship to civil government; widows—the care of widows; prophetesses—the duration of spiritual gifts, etc.

The first lesson, "How God Uses What We Do," is designed to root the theme in your mind. Eight sections follow with the women of the Bible classified for the most part by what they did—or miserably failed to do—to further God's plan.

A section of reviews is located in the back of the book. At the end of each section the students should do the appropriate review in class without discussion or notes of any kind. The women in the section are listed at the top of the review. Each question, though it be worded as if it had one correct answer, may have two, three, or more answers. When everyone in class is finished, the reviews should then be checked in class and discussed. Each review will take an entire class period.

In doing these lessons it will help to know that the questions are based upon the American Standard version. However, various versions should be used as a means of study. The Keil and Delitszch commentaries and the New Bible Commentary: Revised may be helpful to the teacher. Some other study materials are supplied before some of the lessons, but these are by no means exhaustive.

Each teacher will certainly have her own way of conducting the class, but one thing is necessary: NEVER discuss the purpose and example of the woman/women until you have finished the lesson, otherwise, confusion will result as the class gets ahead of itself. These are placed at the top so that you will be able to tell at a glance what each lesson deals with and use them for any future problems you may have. There are probably no more than half a dozen lessons in this book which will require less than two hours preparation.

Special thanks must be given to the young women's class at the Del Rio church of Christ in Tampa, Florida, and the women of the Gibson City church of Christ, Gibson City, Illinois, for their willingness to use these lessons when still in their rough form, and their encouragement in producing this book. Special thanks also to Barbara Matthews, Donna Stone, and Nancy Cobia for their help with the introduction. I owe a special debt of gratitude to Homer Hailey, whose works were such a help to me, and who allowed me to use portions of two of them, his syllabus on Old Testament Poetry and Wisdom and his commentary on The Minor Prophets, as study materials before two lessons.

INTRODUCTION: HOW GOD USES WHAT WE DO

Text: Prov. 16.3,4; Jer. 18.1–6; 2 Tim. 2.20–22; James 1.13–14

SHORT ANSWER:

1. Why did God make everyone? _____

2. To what is God compared? _____

3. To what is Judah (and everyone else, by application) compared? _____
_____

4. What happens if the vessel is marred? _____

5. Of what are we made if we are a vessel unto honor? _____

6. Of what are we made if we are a vessel unto dishonor? _____

7. If we wish to be a vessel of silver or gold, what must we do? _____
_____

TRUE OR FALSE:

8. T F God has a purpose for everyone.

9. T F God molds us as he wishes and we have nothing to do or say about it.

10. T F If we are marred God will use us for something anyway.

11. T F How we are used depends upon what kind of vessel we are.

12. T F Whether our abilities are great or small, as long as we use them to the fullest, God considers us a vessel of silver or gold.

13. T F Since prophecies had to be fulfilled, Judas had no choice about betraying Jesus.

FOR DISCUSSION:

14. Indicate which were vessels of honor and which of dishonor.

   A. **Sarah** bore Isaac as God had promised.

   B. By attempting to seduce Joseph, Potiphar's Wife eventually caused him to be placed in prison, where he came in contact with Pharaoh's servants and then Pharaoh, and became second ruler of Egypt. It was to him Israel came during the famine.

   C. **Esther** became queen of Persia and saved her people.

   D. **Mary** bore Jesus.

   E. **Sapphira** became an example to the early church.

15. What is God's eternal purpose? How were each of the women above used to further that purpose?

I. THE WOMEN OF GENESIS

Genesis is the book of beginnings—not only the beginning of the world and man, but also the beginning of our salvation. God had a plan even before he formed the world (Eph. 1.3–5; 3.11) and it was set in motion in Eden when man fell. Genesis shows us the beginnings of the line of Christ from Adam to Judah. Although the selections depended primarily on the actions of me, these women played an important role, as an encouragement or a hindrance to overcome.

EVE

Text: *Gen. 2.18–25; 3.1–24; 4.25,26; 5.1–5; 1 Cor. 11.3–12; Gal. 3.27–29; 4.4; 1 Tim. 2.13–15*

EXAMPLE: _____

PURPOSE: _____

TRUE OR FALSE:

1. T F Man and Beast were made the same way and out of the same thing.
2. T F Another word for wife is "helpmeet."
3. T F Although woman did have a distinctive name, Eve, the man did not.
4. T F The fruit of the tree of knowledge was good to eat.
5. T F The man and his wife hid from God.
6. T F Woman was not made with the ability to conceive.
7. T F God made clothes for them.
8. T F Adam and Eve were driven from the garden because they had sinned.
9. T F Adam and Eve had three sons and many daughters.
10. T F Adam named all of his sons.

FOR DISCUSSION:

11. Why did God make woman?
12. What does "one flesh" mean?
13. List and explain the curses and prophecies. Find passages to show that they did come about.
14. Explain the line of authority in 1 Cor. 11.
15. What does "beguiled" mean? How was Eve beguiled? If Adam was not beguiled, then how did he fail? How are they both an example to us?
16. How is woman "saved through childbearing?"
17. If woman is subject to man, how can the distinction between them disappear as in Gal. 3?
18. Give several purposes for marriage.
19. In what ways should we be "meet" for our husbands?
20. What does it mean to be created in the image of God?
21. Through which of Eve's sons did God choose to fulfill the promise of Gen. 3.15? Why him?

SARAH

Text: Gen. 11.27–32; 12.1–20; 15.1–4; 16.1–16; 17.9–21; 18.1–15; 20.1–18; 21.1–14; 23.1–20; 24.67; Josh. 24.2,3; Heb. 11.11; 1 Peter 3.3–6

EXAMPLE: _____

PURPOSE: _____

SHORT ANSWER:

1. Who left the Ur of the Chaldees for Canaan? _____
2. Where was their first stop? _____
3. Who remained and who continued on? _____
4. Why did Abram go into Egypt? _____
   Why did he leave? _____
5. Who was Abram's most faithful servant? How did he wish to elevate him?____
   _____
6. Why did Sarai give Hagar to Abram? _____
7. How did this effect her relationship with her handmaid? _____
8. What served as a token of God's covenant with Abraham? _____
9. Why did Abraham leave Gerar? _____
10. What finally caused Abraham to allow Ishmael to leave him? _____
    _____

LISTING:

11. Five ways Sarah showed subjection: _____
12. Sarah's faults: _____
13. Three promises to Abraham in Gen. 12: _____

FOR DISCUSSION:

14. What later Biblical incident does Abraham's sojourn in Egypt parallel?
15. What is the significance of Sarah's name change?
16. Why might Abraham have felt justified in telling Pharoah and Abimelech that Sarah was his sister? Why was he not?
17. What are the similarities and differences in these two incidents? Why might they have tried it twice?
18. Reconcile Sarah's behavior in Gen. 18.9–12 with Heb. 11.11.
19. Why were Abraham and Sarah chosen from among their brethren to carry the line of Christ?

20. How did Abraham and Sarah try to help God provide them with an heir? Whom did God ultimately choose?

21. How are we circumcised today? (See Rom. 2.28,29; Col. 2.11,12)

22. Where in the Bible does God command the husband to keep his wife in subjection? Whose responsibility is it?

23. List passages showing the fulfillment of the three promises to Abraham.

24. What might these promises have meant to Sarah (to a woman, as opposed to Abraham, a man)?

25. How did the religious beliefs of Terah, their father, effect Abraham and Sarah?

26. What does the effect of Sarah's death on Abraham and Isaac say about her as a wife and mother?

REBEKAH

Text: Gen. 22.20–24; 24.1–67; 25.19–34; 26.1–17,34,35; 27.1–28.5; Rom. 9.8–13

EXAMPLE: _____

PURPOSE: _____

SHORT ANSWER:

1. How were Isaac and Rebekah related? _____

2. What did Abraham's servant swear? _____

3. As you read Gen. 24, make a list of all the goodly things referred to in verse 10. _____

4. What was the sign by which the servant would recognize the future wife of Isaac? _____

5. Who seemed to be the head of Bethuel's house? _____

6. What did Rebekah do when she first saw Isaac and found out who he was? _____

7. Why was Rebekah worried over her pregnancy? _____

8. Was there anything miraculous about her pregnancy? _____

9. How did Abimelech discover that Isaac and Rebekah were married? _____

10. Did Rebekah say anything about her marriage to Isaac? _____

11. Was she justified in being partial to Jacob when Isaac was obviously partial to Esau? _____

FOR RESEARCH:

12. Significance of the names given to Jacob and Esau _____

_____

13. Other names they were known by _____

14. Significance of these names _____

FOR DISCUSSION:

15. Why did Abraham refuse to let Isaac leave Canaan?

16. How did Rebekah try to help God?

17. Rebekah actually failed to help God because she misunderstood the prophecy in Gen. 25. What did the prophecy actually mean? How did she misunderstand it? (See Ma;. 1.2ff)

18. How were the lives of Isaac and Rebekah similar to the lives of Abraham and Sarah?

19. How did Paul use Isaac, Jacob, and Esau in Rom. 9? Which son did God choose to carry the line of Christ? Why?

20. What has Rebekah shown us not to do as a mother? How do we sometimes share Rebekah's fault without realizing it?

21. Contrast Rebekah's subjections to her husband with Sarah's.

22. In what ways do we deceive our husbands?

23. Give the significance of Gen. 26.1–4 to this series of lessons.

LEAH AND RACHEL
Text: Gen. 27.46–32.2; 35.16–20

EXAMPLE: _____

PURPOSE: _____

SHORT ANSWER:

1. Why did Isaac send Jacob away? _____

2. How did Jacob meet Rachel? _____

3. Why did he love Rachel more than Leah? _____

4. Why was Leah given to him instead? _____

5. How long did Jacob work before he married Rachel? _____

How long did Jacob work for Rachel? _____

6. What was unusual about the births of some of Jacob's children? _____

_____

7. What did Rachel steal? How did she hide them? _____

8. What did Rachel say when Joseph was born? _____

9. When was her request answered? At what cost? _____

_____

FOR RESEARCH:

10. What are mandrakes? _____

LISTING:

11. Leah's sons _____

12. Rachel's sons _____

13. Bilhah's sons _____

14. Zilpah's sons _____

15. Which woman carried on the genealogy of Christ? _____

FOR DISCUSSION:

16. In what ways did Rachel try to remove the reproach of her barrenness? In which of these ways was she successful?

17. What was the difference in Sarah's reason for giving her handmaid to her husband and Rachel's reason for doing the same?

18. Study the meanings of the names given the children. What does this say about the attitudes of Leah and Rachel?

19. We do not have other wives to make us jealous of our husband's love and time. What other things do we allow to make us jealous?

20. What good examples did Leah and Rachel set?

21. Which woman seems the more admirable?

22. Why did Jacob change the name Rachel had given their last son?

23. What is the significance of Gen. 28.12–15 to this series of lessons?

DINAH

Text: Gen. 29.31–35; 30.17–21; 34.1–31; 49.1–10

EXAMPLE: _____

PURPOSE: _____

SHORT ANSWER:

1. Who was Dinah's mother? _____ Full brothers? _____
   _____

2. Where did Dinah go? _____

3. Who took her? _____

4. What did he ask of his father? _____

5. What did Jacob do? _____

6. What agreement did Dinah's brothers make with her "suitor?" _____
   _____

7. Who violated the agreement? _____ How? _____

8. How did they justify their actions to Jacob? _____

FOR RESEARCH:

9. From various scriptures, how old was Dinah when this occurred? _____

FOR DISCUSSION:

10. What guilt did Dinah have in this matter?

11. Why might Jacob have let his sons handle this matter instead of taking care of it himself?

12. Find Old Testament passages concerning the requirements of the Law of Moses after rape, seduction, and fornication. (We understand that the Law was not in effect at this time, but many practices of this time were carried over into the Law.)

13. Which of Jacob's sons were guiltless in avenging Dinah?

14. What did Simeon and Levi lose as a result of their vengeance? How did Reuben later lose the same thing?

15. What made Simeon and Levi's vengeance so bad?

16. As a result of all this, which of Jacob's sons was allowed to carry the line of Christ?

17. How may a young woman today keep herself from falling into similar circumstances?

TAMAR AND SHUA'S DAUGHTER

Text: *Gen. 38; Deut. 25.5–10; 1 Chron. 2.1–4; Ruth 4.18–22; Mt. 1.1–16*

EXAMPLE: _____

PURPOSE: _____

SHORT ANSWER:

1. What nationality was Shua's daughter? _____

   Who were her sons? _____

2. Why did Er and Onan die? _____

3. What promise did Judah make to Tamar? Did he keep it? _____

   _____

4. How did Tamar disguise herself? _____

5. What price did he offer to pay her? _____

   What did she keep as collateral? _____

6. What punishment did Judah require for Tamar's whoredom? _____

7. Did Judah take Tamar as his wife? _____

FOR RESEARCH:

8. There was no Mosaic Law at this time. However, God later regulated some of the things mentioned in these verses. Where?

   A. Marriage to a Canaanite (why was it a sin?);

   B. Levirate law;

   C. Burning a fornicator;

   D. Other punishments for fornicator.

FOR DISCUSSION:

9. How did Judah contribute to the wickedness of his children?

10. Why wouldn't Judah keep his promise to Tamar?

11. How hard did Judah try to keep his bargain with the harlot?

12. Why were his possessions such good evidence?

13. What is "righteousness?" Why were Tamar's actions "more righteous" than Judah's?

14. Do Tamar's actions make it "righteous" to go to any lengths to get our "fair share?"

15. Why is Tamar mentioned in Ruth and Matthew?

16. Which of Judah's sons carried the line of Christ? Why were his other sons rejected?

II. WOMEN WHO WERE LEADERS

God has at various times allowed women to play a leading role in His plan. Many times a battle has been led, a nation ruled, a race saved by a woman. The following women have in one way or another led all or part of God's people. Their wise counsel, courage, and faithfulness are good examples to us today. Some abused their God-given privilege, and this may also serve as an example to us of the respect we should have for any limitations God has chosen to set upon us.

QUEENS—A SURVEY

Text:
1. General references to queens—Psalm 45.9; S. of S. 6.8,9
2. Queens of Gentile nations—1 Kings 10.1–13; 11.19; Neh. 2.6; Esth. 1.19–22, 2.16–18; Dan. 5.1–12; Acts 8.27
3. Queens of united Israel—1 Sam. 14.50; 2 Sam. 11.26,27; 1 Kings 11.3; 1 Chron. 3.1–9; 1 Kings 7.8; 1 Sam. 18.20,21,27
4. Queens of Israel (10 tribes)—1 Kings 14.1,2; 1 Kings 16.29–31
5. Queens of Judah—1 Kings 15.13; 2 Kings 8.16–29; 11.1–20; 15.2; 23.36; 24.8; Jer. 13.18; 29.2

God's purpose for queens: _____

_____

TRUE OR FALSE:

1. T F "Queen" sometimes refers to the king's chief wife.
2. T F In another sense, "queen" can refer to all the king's wives, but not his concubines.
3. T F The mother of the present king is never the reigning queen.
4. T F In the Bible, the queen was never the sovereign ruler.
5. T F A queen could be put away.
6. T F There is no recorded instance of a queen sitting on the throne with a king.
7. T F A queen could counsel the king.
8. T F Queens were never allowed to represent their country without the king.
9. T F A duty of the queen was to act as hostess.
10. T F The queen was subject to the king's command.
11. T F The only menservants queens had were guards.

FOR RESEARCH:

12. Make a chart of each queen in the above verses, showing her king and country.
13. The Bible uses several different Hebrew words for "queen." What are they? What is the difference in their meanings?
14. Which of the women in the text are not referred to as queens but only as the "king's wife?" Does this have any significance?

FOR DISCUSSION:

15. What duties has God given each civil government? Has God ordained a certain type of government?
16. What are our duties to the civil government?
17. Name several Christians who were in civil government.

MIRIAM

Text: Ex. 2.1–10; 15.19–21; 32.1–6; 6.20; Micah 6.4; Num. 12.1–15; 20.1

EXAMPLE: _____

PURPOSE: _____

SHORT ANSWER:

1. Why was Miriam sent to watch the ark?

2. What did she do when it was found?

3. What gift did God give Miriam?

4. What did Miriam and the women celebrate?

5. Why did Miriam and Aaron speak against Moses?

6. What was the real reason for their displeasure?

MULTIPLE CHOICE:

7. _____ Miriam's father and mother (in that order): **(a)** Levi and Jochebed; **(b)** Jochebed and Amram; **(c)** Amram and Kohath; **(d)** Amram and Jochebed; **(e)** Jochebed and Levi.

8. _____ Miriam's punishment: **(a)** palsy; **(b)** leprosy; **(c)** leprosy and seclusion; **(d)** she could no longer prophesy; **(e)** permanent outcast.

9. _____ Miriam's husband: **(a)** Amram; **(b)** Merari; **(c)** Eleazar; **(d)** she was unmarried; **(e)** his name is not given.

FOR DISCUSSION:

10. What might have happened if Miriam had not spoken to Pharoah's daughter when she did?

11. In the beginning, how was Miriam helpful to the Israelites, especially the women?

12. As a leader, how did Miriam fail in Ex. 32? In Num. 12?

13. How was Moses different from Miriam and Aaron? Did Moses ever see God face to face (See John 1.18; Ex. 33.17–23)

14. How was Miriam's punishment appropriate to her sin?

15. How did the people seem to react to Miriam's sin and punishment? Is there a lesson in this for us?

16. How does the history of Miriam show that God is not a "male chauvinist?"

17. How might we also rebel against God today? (See 1 Sam. 8.7)

DEBORAH AND JAEL

Text: Judges 4,5

EXAMPLE: _____

PURPOSE: _____

SHORT ANSWER:

1. What two positions did Deborah fill? _____

2. Where did she live? _____

3. Whom did Deborah call and why? _____

   _____

4. Why did Deborah go to the battlefield? _____

   _____

5. How were Sisera's chariots "discomfited?" _____

   _____

6. Why did Sisera feel safe with Jael? _____

7. What hospitality did Jael show Sisera? _____

8. What did Sisera tell Jael to do while he slept? _____

   _____

9. What did she do? _____

10. Whom did Jael go to and what did she show him? _____

    _____

11. How did Deborah and Barak rejoice? _____

12. Did Israel have mighty weapons of war? _____

13. Which tribes fought? _____

    Which did not? _____

FOR RESEARCH:

14. From what famous Bible character was Heber a direct (not by marriage, e.g. Moses) descendant? _____

FOR DISCUSSION:

15. What is a judge? What did a judge do?

16. What two things does a prophet do? Where in the text does Deborah do each of these?

17. What about the killing of Sisera? Was it:
    A. The purpose for which God prepared Jael from birth?
    B. Jael trying to help God?
    C. Brought on by the customs of the time and place—a voluntary action which God used?
    D. Something that God causes because He had it prophesied?
18. Did Jael do a great or a wicked deed?
19. What can we learn and apply to the church from 5.2,9?
20. Deborah, by inspiration, rebuked those tribes which had not fought. What does this teach us?
21. In her song, whom does Deborah show sympathy for and why?
22. Harmonize Judges 4.8–10 and Heb. 11.32–34.

PROPHETESSES—A SURVEY

Text: *2 Kings 22; 2 Chron. 34; Neh. 6.10–14; Isa. 8.1–4; Ezek. 13.17–23; Zech.13.1–3; Luke 1.39–45; 2.21–39; Acts 21.7–9; 1 Cor. 12.4–11; 13.1–14.40; Eph. 4.11–16; Rev. 2.18–28*

GOD'S PURPOSE FOR PROPHETESSES: _____

SHORT ANSWER:

1. What did Hilkiah find? _____
2. Why did Josiah send his men to Huldah? _____
   _____
3. What was her message? _____
4. What did Noadiah and the prophets want to do to Nehemiah? _____
   _____
5. What did Isaiah's wife have to do with prophecy? _____
   _____
6. Why were Mary and Joseph in the temple? _____
7. What did Anna say? _____
8. How many prophetess daughters did Philip have? _____
9. What things did Elisabeth bless and why? _____

TRUE OR FALSE:

10. T F Josiah was the king of Israel.

11. T F There were never false prophetesses, only false prophets.

12. T F Nehemiah's life was threatened.

13. T F Anna never married.

14. T F Prophecy was a miraculous spiritual gift given in the early church.

15. T F Prophecy is a miraculous spiritual gift in the church.

16. T F In New Testament times women in the church prophesied.

17. T F In New Testament times women prophesied in the church.

FOR RESEARCH:

18. Make a chart for the prophetesses, Note whether they were true or false, were married, were mothers, were leaders. Synopsize each one's message. Include other prophetesses we have already studied.

19. From your chart, other than obedience, does God require certain limitations in the lives of his servants? How does this conflict with the teaching of certain denominations?

20. What philosophy did Jezebel promote? What other group followed similar teachings?

FOR DISCUSSION:

21. How did the prophetesses in Ezek. 13 corrupt their true purpose?

22. What was the purpose of the prophecy in the early church? If it had a function then, how are we able to function without it today?

23. In what way do we use the apostles and prophets today?

WITCHES—A SURVEY

HOW GOD USED WITCHES: _____

_____

_____

READ EACH GROUP OF PASSAGES AND ANSWER THE QUESTIONS THAT FOLLOW:

• Ex. 7.11; Deut. 18.10,11; 2 Chron. 33.6; Dan. 2.2; Acts 13.6

1. In the Bible another word for witchcraft is _____

• Lev. 19.26–28; 19.31; 20.6,27; Jer. 3.6–10; Ezek. 21.21; 2.4–7, 36,37

2. What is augury? _____

3. What does "to play the harlot after them" mean? _____

_____

4. What are familiar spirits? _____

• Ex. 22.18; Deut. 13.5; 18.9–14; Isa. 8.19; Mal. 3.5

5. What is a necromancer? _____

6. What is Isaiah's argument against witchcraft? _____

_____

READ ALL THESE PASSAGES AND MAKE A LIST OF ALL THOSE WHO PRACTICED SOME FORM OF WITCHCRAFT:

7. Isa. 19.3,11,12; Ex. 7.11,12; 8.17,18 _____

8. Num 22.5–7,16; 23.23; 24.1; Josh. 13.22 _____

9. 2 Kings 9.22 _____

10. Nahum 3.4,5 _____

11. Isa. 47.9–13; Ezek. 21.21,22; Dan. 2.2,10,27 _____

12. Dan. 5.7,15 _____

13. Acts 8.9–11 _____

14. Acts 13.8 _____

15. Acts 16.16 _____

16. Acts 19.13 _____

17. Acts 19.14,15 _____

18. Jer. 10.2 _____

19. Jer. 14.14; 27.9; 29.8,9; Ezek. 13.6–9; 22.28; Micah 3.6–7; Mt. 24.24 _____

_____

READ THESE PASSAGES AND TELL HOW THE BIBLE DESCRIBED WITCHCRAFT:

20. Ezek. 21.29; Zech. 10.2, 2 Thes. 2.9 _____

21. Gal. 5.19,20 _____

22. 1 Sam. 15.23 _____

23. Isa. 44.25 _____

24. What is "divining?" _____

READ THESE PASSAGES AND TELL WHAT SORCERERS USED TO DIVINE:

25. Lev. 20.27; 1 Chron. 10.13; 2 Chron. 33.6; Isa. 8.19; 19.3; 29.4 _____
_____

26. Ezek. 21.21 _____

27. 2 Kings 23.24 _____

28. Hosea 4.12 _____

Manasseh—2 Kings 21.1–19; 2 Chron. 33.1–20

29. From whom did Manasseh pick up his witchcraft? _____

30. What other sins went along with it? _____

31. What was the result? _____

The witch of Endor—1 Sam. 28.7–25; 1 Chron. 10.13,14

32. Who asked her advice? _____

33. How did she divine? _____

34. What form of witchcraft did she use? _____

35. What was her reaction to the ghost? _____

36. What was the result of this episode? _____

FOR RESEARCH:

We have other forms of witchcraft today. What are these, and how can we teach against them?

37. Astrology

38. Spiritism

39. Satanism

40. Exorcism

FOR DISCUSSION:

41. "Breaking a mirror brings seven years bad luck" is an example of augury. What other examples can you think of that we commonly hear?

42. What should a Christian's attitude be towards all sorts of witchcraft?

ATHALIAH AND JEHOSHEBA

Text: *2 Kings 8.16–29; 9.1–28; 11.1–20; 2 Chron. 21; 22; 23*

EXAMPLE: _____

PURPOSE: _____

Note: Since there are two Jehorams in this lesson, we will separate them as Jehoram, king of Judah, and Joram—the shortened form—king of Israel.

MATCHING:

It might help to sit down and draw a family tree from your reading before attempting this section.

1. _____ Athaliah's husband	**A.**	Ahab
2. _____ Athaliah's son	**B.**	Ahaziah
3. _____ Athaliah's father	**C.**	Omri
4. _____ Athaliah's mother	**D.**	Jehoiada
5. _____ Athaliah's grandfather	**E.**	Jehoshaphat, son of Nimshi
6. _____ Athaliah's daughter	**F.**	Jehoram
7. _____ Omri's great-grandson	**G.**	Athaliah
8. _____ Jehu's father	**H.**	Jehoshaphat, son of Asa
9. _____ Jehoram's father	**I.**	Jehosheba
10. _____ Joram's mother	**J.**	Jezebel
11. _____ Joram's sister		
12. _____ Ahaziah's brother-in-law		

SHORT ANSWER:

13. Why did Jehoram die? _____

14. Why did God appoint Jehu king? _____

15. Why was Ahaziah in Israel? _____

16. What did Athaliah do when her son was killed? _____

17. What did this do for her? _____

18. How were Jehosheba and Athaliah related? _____

_____

19. Whom had Jehosheba married? _____

20. How did Jehosheba ruin Athaliah's plans? _____

_____

21. Why was Athaliah allowed to escape from the temple before she was killed?

_____

FOR DISCUSSION:

22. What was Naboth's portion? Why was Joram's body thrown into it?

23. How did Athaliah's parentage effect her? Did this excuse her?

24. How did Jehosheba's parentage effect her? How did she influence the child she raised?

25. What effect did Athaliah have on her husband, son, and country?

26. In what ways might we influence others?

WIDOWS—A SURVEY

GOD'S PURPOSE FOR WIDOWS: _____

I. OLD LAWS:

Job 22.5–11; 31.16,22	Jer. 49.11	Num. 30.9–12
Zech. 7.10	Lev. 22.12,13	Psa. 94.6
Mal. 3.5	Ex. 22.22–24	Prov. 15.25
Mt. 23.14	Luke 20.47	Isa. 10.1,2
Mark 12.40	Jer. 22.3	
Deut. 10.18; 14.28,29; 24.17–21; 25.5—10		

SHORT ANSWER:

1. In Old Testament times how were widows looked upon? _____
_____

2. What was a symptom of injustice in a man? _____

3. Explain a widow's responsibility for vows and pledges. _____
_____

4. What was the penalty for afflicting a widow? _____

5. What benevolence were widows given? _____
_____

6. How did God allow for remarriage of widows in the Old Testament? _____
_____
_____

II. NEW LAWS:

Rom. 7.3	James 1.27
I Cor. 7.39	Acts 6.1–6
1 Tim. 5.3–16	

7. How may a widow under the new covenant remarry? _____
_____

8. How were widows taken care of in the early church? _____
_____

9. What are widows indeed? _____
_____

10. What is the pledge and enrollment that widows indeed were allowed to take?
_____

11. What instructions are given to younger widows? _____
_____

III. EXAMPLES:

1 Kings 17	Ruth	Mark 12.41–44
2 Kings 4.1–7	Luke 2.36,37	Luke 7.11–15
1 Sam. 4.19–22		

LIST ANY SCRIPTURES UNDER SECTIONS I AND II THAT MIGHT APPLY TO THE WIDOWS LISTED BELOW:

12. Naomi _____

13. Ruth _____

14. Widow of Zarephath _____

15. Widow whose sons were nearly sold _____

16. Anna _____

17. Widow who gave two mites _____

18. Widow of Nain _____

19. Phineas' widow _____

20. List any parallels between Old and New Testament passages concerning widows and caring for them. _____
_____
_____
_____
_____

21. Has God's attitude toward a widow of his people changed? _____

FOR DISCUSSION:

22. Explain the difference between 1. Tim 3.4, an elder ruling his own house, and 1 Tim 5.14, younger widows ruling the household.

23. Why might widows be included with women who were leaders?

THE WOMAN OF TEKOA

Text: *2 Sam. 13.37–14.33*

EXAMPLE: _____

PURPOSE: _____

MULTIPLE CHOICE:

1. _____ David desired to see **(a)** Amnon; **(b)** Joab; **(c)** Absalom.

2. _____ **(a)** Absalom; **(b)** Joab; **(c)** David sent the woman of Tekoa to the king.

3. _____ The woman told the kind **(a)** both her sons were dead; **(b)** one son had murdered the other and now his life was in danger too; **(c)** her husband no longer had seed to carry his name and inheritance.

4. _____ The king promised **(a)** the remaining son would not be harmed; **(b)** the murderer would be punished; **(c)** he would personally avenger her son's murder.

5. _____ David saw that **(a)** Joab; **(b)** Absalom; **(c)** he was guilty.

6. _____ Absalom had been hiding in **(a)** Tekoa; **(b)** Jerusalem; **(c)** Geshur.

7. _____ To get Joab's attention Absalom **(a)** burned his field; **(b)** called out to him; **(c)** sent a message.

8. _____ As a result of all this David and Absalom **(a)** were reunited and reconciled; **(b)** said they would never speak to each other again; **(c)** lived happily ever after.

FOR DISCUSSION:

9. Why was Absalom hiding from David?

10. Why did Joab send for this particular woman?

11. How was she similar to the woman in 2 Sam. 20.14-22?

12. Did the woman tell a lie? (Compare 1 Kings 20.35-43; Heb 6.18)

13. Had David ever listened to a story and condemned himself before this particular event?

14. How did the woman's story apply to David?

15. How did David show that he could be honest with himself?

16. How can we tell today if a person is honest with himself, truly seeking to do the right thing?

17. Was Absalom a good boy from then on?

III. MINISTERS AND STEWARDS

A minister is a servant; a steward is one given something of the master's to manage or care for. Each of these women fit in this category, just as each of us should. Everything we have is God's—He has merely placed it in our keeping. Everyone we meet should receive our service—physically, spiritually, or intellectually. There is always something we can do to help. The following women show us how.

MARY AND MARTHA

Text: Mt. 26.6–13; Luke 10.38–42; John 11.1–12.11

EXAMPLE: _____

PURPOSE: _____

SHORT ANSWER:

1. What did Mary do that upset Martha? _____
2. How did she make known her displeasure? _____
3. How did Jesus answer her? _____
4. How long did Jesus tarry when he heard Lazarus was ill? _____
   _____

   What reason is given? _____
5. What did both Mary and Martha say upon his arrival? _____
   _____
6. What finally caused Jesus to weep? _____
7. What two attitudes were shown by the Jews when Jesus wept? ____
   _____

FOR RESEARCH:

8. How long had Lazarus been dead when they arrived? _____
   Taking in mind the distances (see a map and John 10.40 and 1.28) and Jesus'
   statement in John 11.14, if Jesus had left immediately, would Lazarus have
   been alive when he arrived? _____

FOR DISCUSSION:

9. After the above research, explain the statements in John 11.4,15 (John 11.39
   may help).
10. In John 11, the disciples misunderstood Jesus twice. Find and explain these
    passages.
11. Analyze the faith and understanding of Mary and Martha in the following
    incidents:
    A. Mary listening at Jesus' feet
    B. Martha's discussion with Jesus concerning the resurrection
    C. Their statements about what Jesus could have done if he had been there
       when Lazarus was still alive
    D. Martha's objections to moving the stone
    E. Mary anointing Jesus' feet

12. What does Jesus' answer to Martha in Luke 10 say to women today?

13. How does Martha show a good attitude in John 12 considering what had happened before?

14. Were Mary and Martha ministers or stewards? To whom and/or of what?

THE WIDOW OF ZAREPHATH AND THE SHUNEMITE WOMAN

Text: 1 Kings 17; 2 Kings 4.8–37; 8.1–6; Luke 4.24–26

EXAMPLE: _____

PURPOSE: _____

SHORT ANSWER:

1. Why did God send Elijah to Zarephath?

2. What was the widow about to do when he arrived?

3. What miracle was first performed?

4. What terrible thing did the widow think he had caused?

5. What did the Shunemite woman do for Elisha?

6. With what did he repay her?

7. When the famine came what did he tell her to do?

8. What did she lose by doing this?

9. How did she regain it?

FOR RESEARCH:

10. What are modernists? How do they "explain" the following miracles:

    A. Ravens feeding Elijah

    B. Continuing supply of oil and meal

    C. Raising the widow's son

FOR DISCUSSION:

11. In the New Testament miracles were performed to confirm that those who did them were from God and thus spoke the truth. In these verses, why were the following miracles performed:

    A. Continuing the supply of oil and meal

    B. Raising the widow's son

C. Conception by the Shunemite woman

D. Raising the Shunemite's son

12. Why did Elijah ask the widow to use up her last bit of food?

13. What is meant by saying the Shunemite woman was great?

14. When misfortune occurred the widow was ready to pin the blame on Elijah. How was the Shunemite woman like this also? Why?

15. In what ways did the Shunemite woman show her faith/

16. How did Jesus use the widow of Zarephath as an example?

17. From 2 Kings 4.27 what can we learn about the miraculous powers of a prophet?

18. How were these women ministers and/or stewards?

MARY AND ELISABETH

Text: Mt. 1.18–2.23; Luke 1.1–2.52; Mal. 4.5,6; Num. 6.1–5

EXAMPLE: _____

PURPOSE: _____

SHORT ANSWER:

1. What prophet was John to be like? _____

2. What happened to Zaccharias because of his doubt? _____

3. How could the people tell he had seen a vision? _____

4. How did the angel's salutation affect Mary? _____

5. What was Mary's attitude to the news when the angel finished speaking?

6. What did Mary do when the angel left her? _____

7. How did Elisabeth greet Mary? _____

8. Although Elisabeth realized that Mary's child would be the Messiah and her's Forerunner, what was her attitude? _____

9. How did Elisabeth show her loyalty to and support of her husband? _____

10. Mark the things which Jesus and John had in common:

_____ miraculous conception   _____ young mothers

_____ name given by God   _____ prophesied of

_____ birthdate   _____ Deity

_____ Nazirite   _____ birth announced by Gabriel

_____ circumcised the 8th day   _____ people wondered at his birth

_____ certain relatives   _____ angel spoke to father before his birth

_____ trade   _____ angel spoke to mother before his birth

_____ preached   _____ tribe

FOR DISCUSSION:

11. What other couple in the Bible do Zacharias and Elisabeth resemble and in what ways?

12. How was John going to live? What is this lifestyle called? What other people in the Bible lived this way?

13. Why did Elisabeth hide herself?

14. What is the importance of Mary's pondering (Luke 2.19,51)?

15. Considering Jesus' great knowledge of the scripture at such a young age in the same light as his temptations, i.e. as examples of what we can do if we will, what great responsibility is placed upon us as parents?

16. What is involved in the Jewish betrothal?

17. How did Mary and Elisabeth each show their submission to the will of God?

18. How were Mary and Elizabeth ministers and/or stewards?

HANNAH, MANOAH'S WIFE, LOIS AND EUNICE

Text: 1 Sam. 1.1–2.21; 1 Chron. 6.33–38; Judges 13.1–25; 14.1–3; Num. 6.1–5; 2 Tim. 1.3–5; 3.14,15; Acts 16.1–3

EXAMPLE: _____

PURPOSE: _____

I. WHICH OF THE MOTHERS...

1. Was barren? _____

2. Married a Danite? _____

3. Received a double portion? _____

4. Bore timothy? _____

5. Sang a song? _____

6. Prayed for a child? _____

7. Temporarily took the Nazirite vow? _____

8. Was praised by Paul? _____

9. Was thought to be drunken? _____

10. Married Elkanah? _____

11. Spoke with an angel? _____

12. Was one of two wives to the same man? _____

13. Married a Greek? _____

14. Gave her son to be a minister to Jehovah? _____

15. Had a son who became a minister of the Lord? _____

16. Had unfeigned faith? _____

17. Made a coat every year? _____

18. Was mentioned because of her grandson? _____

19. Bore Samson? _____

20. Did not have her son circumcised? _____

21. Lived in Ephraim? _____

22. Bore Eunice? _____

23. Had her womb shut up? _____

24. Bore Samuel? _____

25. Had unfeigned faith first? _____

26. Had a son who took the Nazirite vow? _____

27. Married a Levite? _____

SHORT ANSWER, DISCUSSION, AND RESEARCH:

II. HANNAH

28. What were the portions Elkanah gave his family? _____

29. Elkanah did love Hannah, but what does 1 Sam. 1.6–8 teach us about the nature of men that will help us in dealing with our husbands? _____
_____

30. Did Hannah ever complain about Peninnah's treatment of her? _____

31. What does Hannah teach us about prayer? _____
_____

32. What does Hannah teach us about giving? _____
_____

33. Compare Peninnah and Hannah with Leah and Rachel. _____
_____

III. MANOAH'S WIFE

34. What attitude did Manoah and his wife have toward the will of God that we would do well to imitate? _____

35. Did Manoah and his wife see God? _____

36. How did Manoah's wife use her reasoning ability to ascertain the will of God? Is this privilege in any way limited? _____

37. Why might God have desired Samson's mother to follow the Nazirite vow? _____

IV. LOIS AND EUNICE

38. If Timothy's mother was a Jewess, why didn't she have Timothy circumcised? _____

39. What did Lois and Eunice teach Timothy? _____

40. What can grandmothers learn from Lois? _____

V. FROM EACH WOMAN LIST PRINCIPLES SHE TEACHES US ABOUT RAISING CHILDREN:

41. Hannah

42. Manoah's wife

43. Lois

44. Eunice

45. Of what were all these women stewards? _____

46. How are we stewards in the same way? _____

47. What does this indicate about our parental responsibilities?

THE WOMEN WHO WENT WITH JESUS

Text: Mt. 12.46–50; 27.45–66; 28.1–10; Mark 15.33–47; 16.1–11; Luke 8.1–3; 24.1–21; John 2.1–12; 19.23–27; 20.1–18

EXAMPLE: _____

PURPOSE: _____

LISTING:

1. Make a list of all the women who followed Jesus. Include any other identifying factors—husbands, sons, homes, etc.

TRUE OR FALSE:

2. T F Jesus cared no more for his mother than he did for any other woman.

3. T F None of the women who followed Jesus had families to care for.

4. T F Some of the women who followed Jesus had husbands who likewise believed.

5. T F Only those who were poor followed Jesus.

6. T F Jesus had healed all the women who followed him.

FOR RESEARCH:

7. How does Mormon doctrine view some of these women?

8. What are some of the common but non-Biblical beliefs concerning the identity of Mary Magdalene?

FOR DISCUSSION:

9. Why did Jesus answer his mother as he did in John 2.4?

10. What problems may these women have faced with family and society?

11. What types of things did they do for the Lord? Was any one woman's contribution more essential than another's?

12. Is it feasible for us to do these things today?

13. What other women have we already studied who might be included in this group?

14. What other incident in the ministry of Jesus is Salome noted for? What does this tell us about her (and probably the other women's) understanding of the kingdom?

LYDIA, PRISCILLA, DORCAS, MARY OF JERUSALEM, AND MARY OF ROME

Text: *Acts 9.36–43; 12.1–19; 16.11–15; 16.40; 18.1–3; 18.24–28; Rom. 16.3–6*

EXAMPLE: _____

PURPOSE: _____

SHORT ANSWER:

1. What did the Christians do for Dorcas' body after she died? _____
   _____

   What does this indicate? _____

2. What was the result of her resurrection? _____

3. Where and what was Lydia worshipping? _____

4. What was the occupation of Priscilla and Aquila? _____

5. What did they do for Paul? _____
   _____

6. Why did Paul mention Mary in the Roman letter? _____
   _____

7. What did Mary of Jerusalem do for the church there? _____

MATCHING:

8. _____ Pontus

9. _____ Claudius

10. _____ Thyatira

11. _____ Peter

12. _____ Alexandria

13. _____ Joppa

14. _____ Apollos

15. _____ Simon

16. _____ Prisca

17. _____ Mary

18. _____ Rhoda

19. _____ Tabitha

A. Lydia's home

B. Apollos' home

C. raised Tabbitha

D. mother of John Mark

E. where Peter lodged

F. Dorcas

G. Roman emperor

H. Aquila's home

I. Mary (R)

J. Dorcas' home

K. a good preacher

L. Priscilla

M. answered Peter's knock

FOR RESEARCH:

20. Find out something about Philippi. Why did the women meet by the river?

FOR DISCUSSION:

21. When traveling, how should we follow Lydia's example?

22. Although Lydia was a working woman, what better things did she make time for?

23. How is Priscilla similar to Lydia in the above manner?

24. Why did Apollos need correction? What does Priscilla's role in this tell us?

25. Why did Paul stay with Priscilla and Aquila? Does this mean it is wrong for preachers to receive full support? (Find scriptures to back up your statement.)

26. How is Dorcas an example to bored women at home who "have nothing to do?"

27. What might have been some of the results had these women not used their abilities in the ways they did?

28. Make a list of the ways we can "bestow much labor" on the church.

29. How important is it that we use our abilities? (See 1 Peter 4.7–11; 1 Cor. 4.1,2)

30. To whom were these women ministers? Of what were they good stewards?

IV. YOUNG WOMEN

Age (other than to be accountable before God) is not a prerequisite for carrying out a part of God's plan for we never know how long we may live to serve Him. Some of these young women recognized the opportunities God set before them at an early age and followed through. And if we sometimes feel that God's only use for women was to bear an heir in the genealogy or a preacher, these single or recently married women show us there is much more we can do.

JEPHTHAH'S DAUGHTER

Text: Judges 10.17–11.40; Lev. 18.21; 20.2–5; 27; Deut. 12.31; Jer. 19.1–9

EXAMPLE: _____

PURPOSE: _____

SHORT ANSWER:

1. What people had oppressed Israel at this time? _____

2. Why did Jephthah flee to Tob? _____
_____

3. What did the Israelites promise Jephthah if he would lead them in war? _____
_____

4. What did Jephthah vow? _____

5. What was his daughter's attitude when she learned of the vow? _____
_____

6. What favor did she ask? _____

7. What did she bewail? _____

8. Quote 11.39—the result of Jephthah's vow. _____

FOR RESEARCH:

9. Find various readings of Judges 11.40.

FOR DISCUSSION:

10. What was Jephthah's argument to the king of Ammon? (For related readings see Num. 20.14–21; 21.10–22.1)

11. Compare Judges 11.7,9 with Prov. 1.23–33; Zech. 7.11–13. What can we learn about the difference between man's ways and God's ways?

12. How may a Christian use the story of Jephthah to help him in his life? (See Heb. 11.32–12.13)

    A. What does God think of human sacrifice?

    B. What was the law concerning devoting things to God by a vow?

    C. What restrictions does God place on obedience to parents?

13. Considering the above, Judges 11.39,40, and Jephthah's commendation in Heb. 11, discuss whether Jephthah burned his daughter as a sacrifice or devoted her to God for the rest of her life?

THE DAUGHTERS OF ZELOPHEHAD

Text: Num. 27.1–11; 36.1–13; Josh. 17.1–6

EXAMPLE: _____

PURPOSE: _____

SHORT ANSWER:

1. Who is the best known ancestor of these women? _____

2. How many were there? _____ What were their names? _____

3. How had their father died? _____

4. What did they ask of Moses? _____

5. What new law did God make? _____

6. What new problem did the family heads of Manasseh see because of this law?
   _____

7. What new law was then added? _____

8. Did the daughters follow this law? _____

9. When the Israelites moved into Canaan, what land did Manasseh receive?
   _____ How was it divided? _____

10. Did the daughters of Zelophehad receive their share? _____

FOR DISCUSSION:

10. When God was silent, what was Moses' course of action? Did he do this at any time other than our lesson text?

11. What should be our course of action when God is silent? Cite examples of how we do this.

12. When the daughters saw an unfairness in the law of God toward the women of his people, what did they do? How should we handle any such unfairness in civil law today?

TAMAR

Text: *2 Sam. 13.1–39*

EXAMPLE: _____

PURPOSE: _____

SHORT ANSWER:

1. Who was Tamar's full brother? _____
   What relation was Amnon to her? _____

2. How was Jonadab related to Tamar? _____

3. What "malady" befell Amnon? _____

4. What plan did Jonadab give him? _____

5. What plea did Tamar make to Amnon? _____

6. What were the emotional results of Amnon's actions? _____
   _____

7. How did Absalom comfort his sister? _____

8. What actions did her father take? _____

9. How long did Absalom wait before avenging Tamar? _____

10. What did he do? _____

FOR RESEARCH:

11. 2. Sam 13.12—Find scriptures in the law to show that this was specifically
    prohibited. _____

FOR DISCUSSION:

12. How does this compare with the incident involving Dinah?

13. What sin did David commit immediately before this incident? How might
    these incidents be considered in regard to that sin?

14. What warnings did Tamar fail to see?

15. What was the import and symbolism of Tamar's mourning?

16. If this should happen to a Christian what actions and attitudes would God
    expect of her afterwards?

ESTHER

Text: the book of Esther

EXAMPLE: _____

PURPOSE: _____

CHARACTERS IN THE BOOK:

1. _____ Vashti		**A.**	gate keeper
2. _____ Hegai		**B.**	became drunken
3. _____ Wise men		**C.**	asked to have Vashti put away
4. _____ Haman		**D.**	refused to obey her husband
5. _____ Mordecai		**E.**	was hanged
6. _____ Esther		**F.**	chamberlain
7. _____ Ahasuerus		**G.**	harem keeper
8. _____ Hathach		**H.**	Hadassah

SHORT ANSWER:

9. How long did the feast last? _____

10. Why was Vashti put away? _____

11. How did Hegai show favor to Esther? _____

12 What did Mordecai tell Esther not to do? _____

13. Why was Mordecai's name in the book of chronicles? _____
_____

14. How did Mordecai come into disfavor with Haman? _____
_____

15. What did Haman get the king to do? _____
_____

How did he get him to do it? _____

16. What did Haman's friends tell him about Jews? _____
_____

17. Why was Esther afraid to go before the king? _____
_____

18. What changed her mind? _____

19. What strategy did Esther use in indicting Haman before the king? _____
_____

20. How did Mordecai finally fare in Persia? _____

FOR RESEARCH:

21. What were the "wise men who knew the times?" _____

22. From whom was Haman descended? _____

23. What is the time element in the book of Esther? _____
_____

24. What is the feast of Purim? _____

25. What is the unusual Biblical meaning of "go/went/come in unto" as used in 2.15? _____

FOR DISCUSSION:

26. What was the course of events for each young woman taken into the palace?

27. Who was Zeresh? What kind of wife was she?

28. Cite verses in Esther which tell us the character of Haman by his thoughts and actions.

29. What is the irony in the book of Esther?

30. How does this prove that God may work in the world without miracles?

OUTLINE OF SONG OF SOLOMON

(from Homer Hailey's Old Testament Poetry and Wisdom Syllabus)

PART I—IN THE ROYAL TENTS IN ISSACHAR 1.2–3.5

Scene 1—Shulamite and chorus in tent 1.2-8

- Shulamite 1.2–4a (Draw me…the king has brought me into his chambers)
- Chorus 1.4b (We will run after thee. We will be glad and rejoice, etc.)
- Shulamite 1.5–7 (Except "but comely" by the chorus)
- Chorus 1.8

Scene 2—Shulamite and Solomon in tent 1.9–2.7

- Solomon 1.9–11
- Shulamite 1.12–14
- Solomon 1.15
- Shulamite 1.16–2.1—thinking of her shepherd-lover
- Solomon 2.2
- Shulamite 2.3–7

Scene 3—First song of the Shulamite: reminiscence of her lover's visit 2.8–17

- Shulamite 2.8–10a
- Shepherd 2.10b–15 (She hears him in her thoughts.)
- Shulamite 2.16,17

Scene 4—In a dream the Shulamite seeks and finds her lover. 3.1–5

PART II—THE ROYAL PROCESSION ENTERING JERUSALEM

- Chorus of people 3.6
- First citizen 3.7
- Second citizen 3.8
- Third citizen 3.9,10
- Chorus of people 3.11

PART III—IN THE ROYAL PALACE IN JERUSALEM

Scene 1—Solomon's second effort to woo the Shulamite 4.1–5.1

- Solomon 4.1–5; 7
- Shulamite 4.6
- Shepherd 4.8–15 (She fancies she sees him coming to get her.)
- Shulamite 4.16
- Shepherd 5.1a
- Chorus or Poet (Author) 5.1b (Eat…)

Scene 2—Second dream of the Shulamite and the conversation which follows 5.2–6.3

- Shulamite 5.2–8 (Dreaming she is at home and her beloved visits.)
- Chorus of ladies 5.9
- Shulamite 5.10–16
- Chorus of ladies 6.1
- Shulamite 6.2,3

Scene 3—Solomon's third attempt to woo the Shulamite 6.4–8.4

- Solomon 6.4–9
- Shulamite 6.11,12
- Chorus 6.13a
- Shulamite 6.13b (Why will ye look…)
- Chorus of ladies 7.1–5 (Admiring the dancer)
- Solomon 7.6–9a
- Shulamite 7.9b (interrupting); 7.10 (her final decision); 7.11–8.3 (to her expected lover); 8.4 (to the ladies)

PART IV—IN ISSACHAR—THE SHEPHERD AND THE SHULAMITE, LOVE VICTORIOUS

Scene 1—The shepherd and the Shulamite approaching their mountain home 8.5–7

- Chorus of country people 8.5a
- Shulamite or shepherd (undecided) 8.5b–7

Scene 2—The bride and her brothers 8.8–14

- First brother 8.8
- Second brother 8.9
- Shulamite 8.10–12
- Shepherd-groom 8.13
- Shulamite 8.14

THE SHULAMITE SHEPHERDESS

Text: The Song of Solomon

EXAMPLE: _____

PURPOSE: _____

THESE QUESTIONS COMBINE SHORT ANSWER FROM THE TEXT, RESEARCH, AND DISCUSSION. SOME ARE COMBINATIONS:

1. Give several theories of interpretation of the Song of Solomon. _____
_____
_____

   (The view taken in this lesson is that of the three characters: the shepherd and shepherdess, and Solomon who tries to woo the shepherdess from her lover, but fails.)

2. Why was the Shulamite's skin dark? _____

3. What do "the tents of Kedar" and the "curtains of Solomon" refer to in 1.5?
_____

4. Why does Solomon compare the Shulamite to a horse in 1.9? _____
_____

5. How does the Shulamite contrast her former home with the royal luxury she is surrounded with in the king's tents? Which does she prefer? _____
_____

6. Who is 2.1 speaking of? _____
   Whom do our Catholic friends think it refers to (see #1)? _____
_____

7. How does the Shulamite compare to other women? _____
_____
   How does the shepherd compare to other men? _____
_____

8. What season of the year is depicted in 2.10–13? _____

9. How could the people tell that the coming procession was Solomon's? _____

10. Why did Solomon have "mighty men?" Was he the only king to ever have them? _____

11. How was palanquin "paved with love?" (3.9,10) _____
_____

12. How many espousals had Solomon had? _____

13. Who was Solomon's mother? _____
Had she crowned him king? _____
What also might this "crowning" refer to? (3.11) _____

14. In 4.1–5 what is the meaning of each description? _____
_____
_____
_____

15. For what is the shepherdess praised in 4.12? _____
_____

16. What is the shepherdess' desire after Solomon's second attempt to woo her?
_____

17. Why did the shepherdess in her dream hesitate before opening the door?
_____

18. What did the women of Jerusalem ask the shepherdess? _____
_____

19. Though they were obviously mocking her, how did she answer them? _____
_____

20. What is the shepherdess referring to in 6.11,12? _____

21. What is the shepherdess' final decision? _____

22. What is he significance of "mandrakes" in 7.13? _____
_____

23. Why does she wish the shepherd were her brother? _____
_____

24. How does 8.5b relate to 2.7; 3.5; and 8.4? _____
_____

25. What things are taught in 8.6,7? _____
_____

26. How did her brothers decide to protect the shepherdess when she was young (when she had "no breasts")? _____
_____

27. What did the shepherdess refuse to do with her "vineyard?" _____
_____

28. What divine principles does the Song of Solomon teach us about romantic love? _____
_____

29. What purpose does the Song of Solomon serve in the Bible? _____
_____

VIRGINS—A SURVEY

GOD'S PURPOSE FOR VIRGINS: _____

I. OLD LAWS: EX. 22.16,17; LEV. 21.10,14; DEUT. 22.13–29

1. If a man believed that his bride was not a virgin, what could he do?
_____

2. If he were mistaken what happened to him? _____

3. Why would he be punished for accusing an innocent girl? _____
_____

4. If he were proven correct what happened to the girl? _____
_____

5. How was a virgin expected to react if she were attacked? _____
_____

6. The bride of a high priest was always a _____. He could not
marry a _____ or a _____ woman.

II. NEW SUGGESTIONS: 1 COR. 7.8,9; 25–38

7. Explain 1 Cor. 7.9. _____

8. Why did Paul discourage marriage? _____
_____

9. What general rule did he set forth regarding whether or not to marry?
_____

III. FIGURATIVE USES: ISA. 62.5; JER. 14.17; 31.4,13; 2 COR. 11.2

10. How is "virginity" used figuratively in both the old and new testaments?
_____

11. What seems to be the modern attitude toward both spiritual and figurative virginity? _____

12. What should our attitude be? _____

IV. EXAMPLES

Jephthah's daughter: Judges 11.29–40   Rhoda: Acts 12.15–16

Naaman's servant: 2 Kings 5.1–4   Dinah: Gen. 34

Daughters of Zelophehad: Num. 27   Esther: (chapter 2 only)

Philip's daughters: Acts 21.8,9   Tamar: 2 Sam. 13.1–19

Shulamite shepherdess: Song of Solomon

*Beside each young woman listed above, write down what good or bad examples she set
for our young women today.*

V. DOUBLE STANDARD?

13. Find passages showing that there is no double standard in the church regarding the virginity of both men and women. _____

_____

14. To whom and concerning what does Prov. 7 apply? _____

_____

FOR DISCUSSION:

15. According to Paul's reasoning, who may do a better work, a married preacher or a single preacher? What do our practices today indicate?

16. How may a single woman be "more careful for the things of the Lord?"

GENTILE WOMEN

We have in this section proof that God was indeed the God of the Gentiles (Rom. 3.29), even though they did not obey him and were rejected as a people. For in these lessons we see how God used their unwitting and evil actions to further his plan. And occasionally we find a woman who "clearly saw" the "invisible things" (Rom. 1.18–23), believed God and obeyed him, and was received as his child.

HAGAR

Text: Gen. 16; 17; 21.1–21; 25.12–18; Gal. 4.21–31

EXAMPLE: _____

PURPOSE: _____

SHORT ANSWER:

1. Who was Hagar? What was her nationality? _____

2. How long after the original promise (Gen. 12) did Sarah wait before giving Hagar to Abraham? _____

3. How did Hagar react when she became pregnant? _____
_____

4. Why did Hagar flee? _____

5. What did the angel tell her to do? What promises did he make? _____
_____

6. How old was Abraham when Ishmael was born? _____
How old was Ishmael when Isaac was born? _____

7. Why did Sarah want to cast Ishmael out? _____

8. Why didn't Abraham want him to go? _____

9. Why did Hagar leave Ishmael under a bush? _____

10. What promise concerning Ishmael did God make to Abraham? Where in the Scriptures do we find its fulfillment? _____
_____

FOR RESEARCH:

11. The angel told Hagar that Ishmael would be a "wild ass among men" (16.12). In the light of Job 24.5 and 39.5–8, what might this have meant to her? What indications are given that this prophecy was fulfilled?

12. What does it mean for Sarah to be "despised" in Hagar's eyes? How did Sarah act when the tables were turned in Gen. 21?

FOR DISCUSSION:

13. Why was Ishmael rejected from being in the line of Christ? After his separation from Abraham, how is this rejection shown even further?

14. Although rejected, why was God with Ishmael? How far will God go in blessing those who are dear to his children?

15. What might have been the reason for Hagar's choosing Ishmael a wife out of Egypt?

16. How does Paul use Hagar and Sarah in Gal. 4?

RAHAB

Text: Josh. 2; 6.12–27; Heb. 11.30,31; Hames 2.24–26

EXAMPLE: _____

PURPOSE: _____

SHORT ANSWER:

1. Where did Rahab live? _____
2. What was her occupation? _____
3. What did Rahab tell the king's men? _____
4. Where did she hide the spies? _____
5. Why did Rahab help the men? _____
6. What did Rahab do in 2.11 that everyone must do regarding Jesus before they can become a Christian? (see Acts 8.37) _____
   _____
7. Where was her house located? _____
8. How were the Israelites to know her house when they returned? _____
   _____
9. What did the Israelites do for Rahab in return for her help? _____
   _____

FOR RESEARCH:

10. Who tried to rebuild Jericho? _____
    Did Joshua's prophecy come true? _____

FOR DISCUSSION:

11. Why would the men choose to go into the house of a harlot?
12. Was Rahab's lie justified?
13. How did the Israelites use the town of Jericho after they conquered it? Why?
14. Rahab was put outside the camp because she was a Gentile. Was she every fully accepted by the Jews?
15. How does the New Testament use Rahab as an example for Christians today? For alien sinners?
16. Explain how Rahab could have been justified by both faith and works.

RUTH, ORPAH, AND NAOMI

Text: the book of Ruth

EXAMPLE: _____

PURPOSE: _____

MATCHING:

1. _____ Mahlon	**A.** Naomi's grandson
2. _____ Chilion	**B.** a Gentile nation
3. _____ Orpah	**C.** Orpah's husband
4. _____ Boaz	**D.** Bethlehem
5. _____ Elimilech	**E.** Ruth's descendent
6. _____ Mara	**F.** Ruth's husband
7. _____ Moab	**G.** turned back
8. _____ Ephrath	**H.** Naomi
9. _____ Obed	**I.** Naomi's husband
10. _____ David	**J.** Elimilech's kinsman

SHORT ANSWER:

11. Why did Elimilech leave Israel? _____

Why did Naomi return? _____

12. Why did Orpah go back to Moab? _____

13. How did Boaz show his good favor toward Ruth in the gleaning field? _____

_____

On the threshing floor? _____

Ruth has been praised for many things. Below is given a list of many of the good qualities that have been ascribed to her. Choose a characteristic from the list and match it to one of the good works mentioned that she performed. Then make note of a similar work we might perform to show the same characteristic.

faith	modesty	diligence	love
virtue	obedience	courage	humility

14. Ruth left her own country to go to Israel 1.16,17 _____

_____

15. Ruth worked all day for her mother-in-law and herself 2.7 _____

_____

16. Ruth followed her mother-in-law's instructions 3.6 _____

_____

17. Ruth did not seek after younger men 3.10 _____

_____

18. Ruth followed Boaz's instructions so as to protect her reputation 3.14 _____

_____

19. Ruth bowed before Boaz 2.10 _____

20. Ruth recognized her unequal status as a Gentile and did not complain 2.13

_____

21. Ruth accepted Jehovah rather than the idols that her people worshipped 1.16

_____

FOR RESEARCH:

22. When did these events occur in relation to other Bible events?

23. Under the law, Boaz took responsibility as the redeemer for Ruth and Naomi. Find passages to explain this.

FOR DISCUSSION:

24. Of the above qualities that Ruth had, which did Orpah have and what did she definitely lack?

25. What problems might Ruth have faced in moving from Moab to Israel? What similar problems do we face in moving from the world to the church?

26. Why was Boaz the one they chose to approach for marriage?

27. What things did Naomi do for Ruth that every mother-in-law should seek to do for her daughter-in-law?

28. Knowing that becoming one of God's people was Ruth and Orpah's only hope of salvation, why would Naomi try to get them to stay in Moab?

29. Naomi left all she had when she entered Moab because of the famine, yet she said she "went out full." To what was she referring? What does this tell us about her sense of values?

QUEEN OF SHEBA

Text: 1 Kings 10.1–13; 2 Chron. 9.1–12; Mt. 12.42

EXAMPLE: _____

PURPOSE: _____

SHORT ANSWER:

1. Why did the Queen of Sheba come to see Solomon? _____
_____

2. What did Solomon tell her? _____

3. What did she see at Solomon's court? _____
_____

4. Did she know anything about Jehovah? _____

5. What did she give Solomon? _____

6. What did he give her? _____

FOR RESEARCH:

7. Where was Sheba?

8. What does traditional history say about Solomon and Sheba? Is there any evidence of this from the scriptures?

FOR DISCUSSION:

9. About what did Jesus commend the Queen of Sheba?

10. In what way would she "judge" that generation? In what way does she "judge" us today?

11. Find passages that tell us how to be wise.

POTIPHAR'S WIFE

Text: Gen 37.12–36; 39; 41.1–46; 45.1–11; Psalm 105.16–24; Acts 7.8–14

EXAMPLE: _____

PURPOSE: _____

SHORT ANSWER:

1. To whom did his brothers sell Joseph? _____

2. Why did they sell him? _____

    Did God cause them to sell him (Psalm 105.17)? _____

3. How did Potiphar favor Joseph? _____

4. How did he show his confidence in him? _____

_____

5. Why did Potiphar's wife favor Joseph? _____

6. How did Joseph answer his temptress? _____

_____

7. What further measures did he take to keep from sinning? _____

_____

8. Where in prison was he placed? _____

9. Why did the keeper of the prison favor Joseph? _____

10. How did he show his confidence in him? _____

FOR DISCUSSION:

11. As a servant, how could Joseph be prosperous (39.2)? As servants of God, how can we be prosperous?

12. Did Potiphar believe in Jehovah?

13. Compare Prov. 7 with Gen. 39. How does the Bible describe a man who falls into this trap? Discuss the application of Mt. 5.27,28.

14. Why did Potiphar's wife conspire against Joseph when he refused her? What tactics did she use to get even?

15. Knowingly or not, we sometimes use unfair tactics with brethren and people of the world. What kinds of things should we be careful to avoid in our dealings with others, particularly when we have been hurt or experience a personality conflict?

16. Is there any real difference between the actions of Potiphar's wife and those of Amnon in 2 Sam. 13?

17. Compare and reconcile Gen. 39.14; 41.13; and Acts 7.13. If Joseph's race were already known, how could it have been "made manifest" to Pharoah?

18. Did God cause Potiphar's wife to sin? How did He use her?

19. What examples does Joseph give in facing temptations? Where are these principles which he exemplifies recorded in the New Testament?

20. Potiphar's wife gives us several examples of the methods Satan uses in "seeking to devour" us. What are they?

JEZEBEL

Text: 1 Kings 16.29–33; 17.1–18.19; 21.1–29; 22.1–40; 2 Kings 1.1–17; 9.1–10.14

EXAMPLE: _____

PURPOSE: _____

SHORT ANSWER:

1. Whom did Jezebel marry? _____

2. What was her nationality and religion? _____

3. What natural event did Elijah prophesy? _____

4. How had Obadiah shown his fear of the Lord? _____

5. Why did Naboth refuse to sell his vineyard to Ahab? (See Lev. 25.23–28; Num. 36.1–9) _____

6. How did Jezebel get the vineyard? _____

7. What did Jehu consider his duty? _____

8. What three things did Elijah predict about Ahab and his family? Where in the scriptures do we find the fulfillment of each? _____

TRUE OR FALSE:

9. T F Marrying Jezebel was one of the worst sins Ahab committed.

10. T F Jezebel never followed Jewish law.

11. T F Jezebel jumped out of a window.

12. T F Even though evil, Jezebel was respected because of her position.

FOR DISCUSSION:

13. What in these and other passages makes Elijah a special prophet?

14. Why was marrying Jezebel such a sin?

15. What good qualities did Jezebel possess and how did she use them for evil? (For example: she was very religious)

16. Why didn't Jezebel just have Naboth executed in the first place?

17. What is ironic about the results of the battle in 1 Kings 22?

18. Who was Zimri? Why did Jezebel call Jehu Zimri in 2 Kings 9.31?

19. As evil as she was, how could God have possibly used Jezebel to further his eternal plan?

THE SAMARITAN WOMAN
Text: John 4.1–42

EXAMPLE: _____

PURPOSE: _____

SHORT ANSWER:
1. Why did Jesus leave Judea? _____
2. Why was Jesus alone? _____
3. What time of day was it? _____
4. Why did the woman think Jesus was a prophet? _____
5. Why did his disciples marvel? _____
6. Who taught the other Samaritans? _____

FOR RESEARCH:
7. Find Old Testament background for verses 5, 6, 12.
8. Why did Jews have no dealings with Samaritans?
9. What mountain did the fathers worship in?
10. Why did the Jews worship in Jerusalem?

FOR DISCUSSION:
11. What is the "gift of God" in verse 10?
12. How did the Samaritans worship "that which they knew not?"
13. Who are the "others" in verse 38?
14. Why did the Samaritans believe on Jesus? Why do we believe on Jesus?
15. What principles for doing personal work can we learn from Jesus' approach to the Samaritan woman?

DELILAH AND THE WOMAN OF TIMNAH

Text: *Judges 13.24–16.31*

EXAMPLE: _____

PURPOSE: _____

SHORT ANSWER:

1. Why did Samson's parents object to his marrying the Timnite woman? _____
    _____
    _____

    Were they lawfully right to object? _____
2. What was the riddle Samson put forth and what did it mean? _____
    _____
3. With what did the thirty companions threaten Samson's wife? _____
    _____

    Of what did they accuse her at the same time? _____
4. How did she persuade Samson to tell her the answer to the riddle? _____
    _____
5. To whom was Samson's wife given? Why? _____
6. How did Samson feel about Delilah? _____
7. Why did Delilah betray Samson? _____
8. What things did Samson say would weaken him? _____
    _____
9. Why did Samson finally tell her his secret? _____

TRUE OR FALSE:

10. T F The Philistines never carried out their threat against the Timnite and his daughter.
11. T F Delilah was by occupation a harlot.
12. T F Delilah was a Philistine.
13. T F Delilah is an example of a nagging wife.
14. T F When Samson's hair was long, he was strong at all times.
15. T F In the end, Samson regained his strength because his hair grew back

FOR DISCUSSION:

16. Did God want Samson to marry the Timnite woman and break the law?
17. What other things has God permitted and legislated, but not approved of?

18. How were Delilah and the woman of Timnah alike?

19. Identify the Spirit which worked in Samson. Did he always have his miraculous strength or only when "inspired?" Did prophets always have miraculous knowledge, or only when inspired (see 2 Kings 4.27)? Was every word and deed of the New Testament writers inspired (see Gal. 2.11–13)?

20. How did the Timnite woman fail as a wife, especially in regard to Gen 2.20 and 1 Peter 3.6?

21. What did these women fail to understand about true love (see S. of S. 8.7)?

THE HERODIAN DYNASTY

Herod the Great

Doris	Mariamne I	Mariamne II	Malthace	Cleopatra
m. 42 BC	m. 37 BC–executed 29 BC	m. 24 BC	m. 23 BC	m. 22 BC

Antipater
Executed 4 BC

Alexander
Executed 7 BC

Aristobulus
Executed 7 BC
m. Bernice

Herod Philip I
d. circa 34 AD
m. Herodias
Mt 14.3; Mk 6.14
Luke 3.19

Archelaus
b. 22 BC; d. 6 AD
Mt 2.2

Herod Antipas
b. 20 BC; d. 39 AD
m. Herodias
Mat 14.1–11; Mk 6.14–28;
Mk 8.15; Lk 3.1; Lk 9.7–9;
Lk 13.31–33; Lk 23.7–15;
Acts 4.37; 13.1

Philip II
d. 34 AD
Luke 3.1

Herod III of Chalcis
d. 48 AD
m. Bernice

Herodias
b. 8 BC
m1. Philip I
m2. Herod Antipas
Mt 14.3–6
Mk 6.17; Lk 3.19

Herod Agrippa I
d. 44 AD
m. Cypros
Acts 12.1–24

Herod Agrippa II
b. 27 AD; d. 100 AD
Acts 25.13–26.32

Bernice
m1. Herod of Chalcis
m2. Polemo of Cilicia
m3. Herod Agrippa II
Acts 25.13, 23; 26.30

Drusilla
m. Felix the Procurator
Acts 24.24

Salome
m. Philip II
Mt 14.6–11; Mk 6.22–28

Although accounts vary, the Herods are generally thought to be of Idumaean descent (Edomites). Drusilla was the daughter of Herod Agrippa I and Cypros. She was at first betrothed to Antiochus Epiphanes, then married to Azizus, king of Emesa. Later she left him for Felix, the procurator of Judea, who paid Simon the Sorcerer to seduce her away from her husband. They had a son named Agrippa. Mother and son died in the eruption of Mt. Vesuvius. Bernice was the eldest daughter of Herod Agrippa I. She married her uncle Herod, king of Chalcis, and after he died became involved in an incestuous relationship with her brother Agrippa II. The she married Polemon, king of Cilicia, but returned to her brother. Later she became the mistress of Vespasian and his son Titus. Herodias was the daughter of Aristobulus. She at first married her uncle Philip, but then left him for another uncle, Antipas. She and Philip had a daughter, Salome, who is thought to have been the one who danced before Antipas and asked for John's head.

DRUSILLA AND BERNICE

Text: *Acts 24.1–9; 24–27; 25.13–26.32*

EXAMPLE: _____

PURPOSE: _____

FOR RESEARCH:

1. How were Agrippa, Drusilla, and Bernice related? _____

2. Who was their forefather from patriarchal times? _____

3. What were some of the sins they committed? _____

4. Although Gentile by race, what was their religion? How can we tell this from scripture? _____

SHORT ANSWER:

5. What were the things Felix hear when Paul spoke to him "concerning the faith in Christ Jesus?" _____

6. What effect did this have on Felix? _____

7. Did he ever call for Paul again? _____

8. Why did Festus want Agrippa and Bernice to hear Paul? _____

9. What charges had the Jews brought against Paul? _____

10. Of what did Festus accuse Paul? _____

11. What was Agrippa's reaction to Paul's defense? _____

12. What did Agrippa, Bernice, and Festus decide about Paul? _____

FOR DISCUSSION:

13. Why should preaching "of righteousness, temperance, and judgment to come" have caused Felix to tremble? How should the preaching of the gospel effect us?

14. What does 26.6 refer to, and what is the irony of 26.7?

15. If Agrippa had become a Christian, what works "worthy of repentance" would he have had to do? Bernice? Drusilla?

16. How did Drusilla and Bernice fail as leaders of women?

HERODIAS AND HER DAUGHTER

Text: Mt. 14.1–12; Mark 6.14–29; Luke 3.18–20; John 10.40–42

EXAMPLE: _____

PURPOSE: _____

FOR RESEARCH:

1. Who was Herod Antipas' father? _____

2. How were Herod Antipas and Herodias related? _____

SHORT ANSWER:

3. When people heard of Jesus' miracles how did they explain it? _____
   _____

4. What sin did John accuse Herod and Herodias of? _____

5. How did Herodias react to John's preaching? _____

6. How did Herod react to John's preaching? _____

7. What did Herodias' daughter do to earn anything "unto half the kingdom?"
   _____

TRUE OR FALSE:

8. T F John rebuked Herod for only one thing.

9. T F John never did a miracle.

10. T F John preached a nicer sermon to Herod than he did to Herodias.

11. T F Herod had put John in prison before his party.

12. T F Only men had been invited to his party.

13. T F Herodias sent her daughter to dance hoping to get a chance to get rid of John.

14. T F Herod kept his promise because he was a man of his word.

FOR DISCUSSION:

15. Compare Herodias with Jezebel.

16. Read Eph. 5.25, 6.1–3, and Mark 6.17, Mt. 14.8 and comment.

17. Compare Herod's reaction to John's preaching with Felix and Agrippa's reaction to Paul's. What did they lack?

18. Why was Herod "much perplexed" with John's preaching?

19. How did Herod know John was a righteous and holy man? How can we know this about anyone?

VI. WIVES

As wives, God has a secondary purpose for our lives. Besides furthering His plan, we are helpers to our husbands. We are to strive to be meet for their needs, and in doing this we will in either a large or small way, do what God had in mind for us. Though we cannot advise one of God's chosen or otherwise aid in the coming of Christ, we can learn from the examples these women set how to help our men to their own salvation and how not to deter them. As you study, keep in mind other wives we have studied in other sections, and compare their actions with those of these women and your own. Do you act as a stepping-stone on your man's way to Heaven, or are you his stumbling block?

ABIGAIL AND MICHAL

Text: 1 Sam. 18.1–21; 19.8–24; 25.2–44; 2 Sam. 3.1–21; 6.16–23

EXAMPLE: _____

PURPOSE: _____

TRUE OR FALSE:

1. T F David married two of Saul's daughters.
2. T F Michal told Saul that David threatened her.
3. T F Nabal was a Gentile.
4. T F Nabal's servants respected him.
5. T F Abigail loved Nabal.
6. T F Abigail asked David to remember her.
7. T F Abigail never told Nabal she had helped David.
8. T F Abigail was David's third wife.
9. T F Michal's second husband did not want to give her up.
10. T F Michal was probably barren.

SHORT ANSWER:

11. Why did Saul want to give a daughter to David? _____

12. What gifts did Abigail give to David's army? _____

13. What good advice did Abigail give David? _____

14. How many wives did David have by the time of 2 Sam. 3? _____

15. Why did Michal get upset with David? _____

FOR RESEARCH:

16. Find other examples of polygamy in the scriptures.
17. Find passages forbidding it and passages legislating it.

FOR DISCUSSION:

18. Why did Nabal turn David away?
19. Why did Abigail not question David's hasty proposal?
20. What other wives did David have? What problems did these women have to face as members of a harem?

21. Why do you think David wanted Michal back?

22. Which of David's wives was probably his best wife? In what ways?

23. Do we have the right to correct our husbands? What was wrong with Michal's correction of David?

BATHSHEBA

Text: 2 Sam. 3.2–5; 11; 12.1–25; 1 Kings 1.1–2.25

EXAMPLE: _____

PURPOSE: _____

MATCHING:

1. _____ Uriah		**A.**	Bathsheba's father
2. _____ Joab		**B.**	Solomon
3. _____ Nathan		**C.**	Bathsheba's husband
4. _____ Solomon		**D.**	David's wife
5. _____ Eliam		**E.**	Solomon's brother
6. _____ Jedidiah		**F.**	Bathsheba's son
7. _____ Abishag		**G.**	priest
8. _____ Haggith		**H.**	prophet
9. _____ Adonijah		**I.**	David's nurse
10. _____ Abiathar		**J.**	captain
11. _____ Zadok			

TRUE OR FALSE:

12. T F Bathsheba was a Jew.

13. T F The adultery was an unconsidered act of passion.

14. T F In the beginning only David and Bathsheba knew she had conceived by him.

15. T F David was not sorry the child died.

16. T F David took his nurse as his wife.

17. T F Adonijah planned to kill Bathsheba and Solomon.

18. T F Adonijah felt like he had been cheated out of the kingdom.

19. T F Bathsheba bowed before her son the king.

SHORT ANSWER:

20. How did David try to cover up the sin? _____

_____

21. Why did Uriah sleep at the door of the king's house? _____

_____

22. How did Joab and David communicate without giving away their secret?

_____

23. How did Nathan know of the sin? _____

LISTING:

24. All the sins involved and what led to each one.

FOR DISCUSSION:

25. From the above list, what conclusions can you draw about sin?

26. Was Bathsheba at all responsible for the sin? If so, how could she have avoided the situation?

27. Are children accountable for their fathers' sins?

28. Analyze Nathan's parable telling who or what each element represents.

29. Why did Adonijah's request to Solomon merit death?

SOLOMON'S WIVES

Text: 1 Kings 3.1–3; 7.1–8; 9.15–19; 11.1–13; Deut. 7.1–11; 17.14–17; Neh. 13.23–27

EXAMPLE: _____

PURPOSE: _____

SHORT ANSWER:

1. Why did Solomon marry Pharoah's daughter? _____

2. What was Solomon's attitude toward God at this time? _____

_____

3. What did Solomon do for Pharoah's daughter? _____

4. How many and what kind of wives did Solomon marry? _____

_____

5. What happened when Solomon was old? Why? _____

_____

6. Did Solomon's wisdom keep him from sin? _____

7. Give the definition of "concubine."

8. What laws did Solomon break?

9. Can anyone today be wiser than Solomon was? If so, how might they evidence this wisdom?

10. These women voluntarily served no purpose for God. But if they had been servants of God, what specific purposes might they have been in a position to fill?

JEROBOAM'S WIFE

Text: 1 Kings 11.26–43; 12.19,20,25–33; 13.33,34; 14.1–18

EXAMPLE: _____

PURPOSE: _____

MULTIPLE CHOICE:

1. _____ Jeroboam was the king of (a) Judah; (b) Egypt; (c) northern ten tribes; (d) none of the above.

2. _____ Jeroboam was from the tribe of (a) Joseph; (b) Ephraim; (c) Judah; (d) none of the above.

3. _____ Jeroboam's becoming king was prophesied by (a) Elijah; (b) Abijah; (c) neither; (d) both.

4. _____ Rehoboam was (a) Jeroboam's second cousin; (b) Solomon's son; (c) Jeroboam's brother; (d) King of Israel.

5. _____ Jeroboam's wife was (a) Nadab; (b) Zeredah; (c) Zeruah; (d) we do not know her name; (e) none of the above.

SHORT ANSWER:

6. Why did Jeroboam send his wife to the prophet? _____

_____

7. What instructions did Jeroboam give her? _____

_____

8. Could the prophet have known her through natural means? _____

_____

9. What did the prophet tell her? _____

_____

10. What symbols were used in the prophecy to Jeroboam? What did they represent?

11. Did God keep his promise to Jeroboam (1 Kings 11)? How did God keep his promise to Jeroboam's wife (1 Kings 14)? How were the two promises related?

12. What things did Jeroboam "devise of his own heart?" How are men guilty of that today?

13. Why did Jeroboam wish to keep his wife's identity a secret? How might Gal. 6.7 apply in this case?

14. How do we try to disguise ourselves before God?

15. At what other times has God punished men by taking their children? Does God work in this way today?

SAPPHIRA

Text: *Acts 4.32–35; 5.1–11, 29*

EXAMPLE: _____

PURPOSE: _____

SHORT ANSWER:

1. Why were Christians selling their possessions? _____
_____

2. Where did people bring their offerings? _____

3. What did Peter say Ananias and Sapphira had done? _____
_____

4. Why did Sapphira come looking for her husband? _____

5. What effect did their deaths have upon the church? _____
_____

TRUE OR FALSE:

6. T F The offering was voluntary.

7. T F Ananias and Sapphira sinned in not giving all.

8. T F Sapphira was guilty even though she knew nothing about it.

9. T F Peter gave them a chance to confess.

10. From this example, how can we lie to the Holy Spirit?

11. How can we use this as a lesson in giving?

12. Did Sapphira go along with Ananias as a matter of subjection or will? Is subjection ever an excuse for sin?

13. What does "tempt the Holy Spirit" mean? How do we do this?

GOMER

Hosea 1–3 Outline and comments from Homer Hailey's Minor Prophets

1.2–9 The prophet's marriage to Gomer by divine command, and the birth of three children to whom were given prophetic names. The picture is one of apostasy and whoredom.

1.10–2.1 Restoration of the children of Israel and the children of Judah to Jehovah.

2.2–7 Jehovah addresses the sinful nation, charging it with spiritual whoredom, having played the harlot. Judgment is threatened.

2.8–13 Jehovah's address continued. The nation will be put in shame before her lovers. The day of the baalim will be visited upon her.

2.14–20 In spite of rejection and punishment, God would bring Israel back to Himself. Under a new covenant He would betroth himself in righteousness and truth.

2.21–23 The new nation will be sown to Jehovah in the earth, filled with all fulness in Him. Those who were not his people, who had not obtained mercy, will now be his people, having obtained mercy.

3.1–5 The prophet tells of his second symbolic marriage in which he buys Gomer back to himself. As Israel would be without the essentials of true worship for a period, so Gomer would not enjoy conjugal relations for a time.

GOMER
Text: *Hosea 1–3*

EXAMPLE: _____

PURPOSE: _____

SHORT ANSWER:

The parallel:

1. Whom does Hosea represent? _____

2. Whom did he marry? _____

3. Whom does she represent? _____

4. Define the names of their three children. What do these names show about Hosea and Gomer? About God and Israel? _____
   _____
   _____
   _____

5. Who were Israel's lovers? _____

6. Did Hosea take Gomer back? _____ Did God take Israel back? _____

7. How was the redeemed Gomer treated for a time? _____
   _____

8. How was redeemed Israel treated for a time? _____
   _____

General questions from the text:

9. Whom did Israel think gave her her blessings? _____

10. What would God do to prove they came from him? _____
    _____

11. After her punishment how would he treat her? _____

FOR RESEARCH:

12. Why would God avenge the slaughter of Ahab's family upon the house of Jehu?

13. When did Israel's name change to Ammi and Ruhammah? (1.10–2.2,23; 1 Peter 1.1; 2.10; Rom. 9.26)

14. 2.14–16 uses deliverance from Egyptian bondage to parallel deliverance from their present bondage. Explain the complete parallel using other Old Testament passages also.

FOR DISCUSSION:

15. How does 1.6,7 show us that God's plan for saving the line of Christ is still on his mind, even in the face of Israel's disobedience?

16. Apply God's stripping of Israel to the stripping of spiritual things (2.2,3).

17. What lessons can Gomer teach us as wives?

18. How can Gomer apply to the church as well as to Israel?

THE LEVITE'S CONCUBINE
Text: *Judges 19–21; Hosea 9.9; 10.9*

EXAMPLE: _____

PURPOSE: _____

TRUE OR FALSE:

1. T F The concubine left the Levite of her own volition.

2. T F The Levite did not want the concubine back.

3. T F The concubine's father was glad to meet the Levite.

4. T F The Levite spent four nights with his father-in-law.

5. T F Jebus was a city of Israel.

6. T F The people of Benjamin were not hospitable to the Levite.

7. T F The Levite said all Benjamites were guilty of murder.

8. T F The war lasted three days with Benjamin winning the most battles.

9. T F God did not guide Israel at this time.

10. T F Benjamites never had Israelite wives again because of the oath.

11. T F Israel had sympathy for Benjamin.

MULTIPLE CHOICE:

12. _____ The murder took place in **(a)** Mizpah; **(b)** Gibeah; **(c)** Jebus.

13. _____ The Levite cut the body into **(a)** 4; **(b)** 10; **(c)** 12 pieces.

14. _____ The 700 men from Gibeah were **(a)** Left-handed; **(b)** base; **(c)** good with a sling.

15. _____ **(a)** Judah; **(b)** Ephraim; **(c)** Reuben led the battle.

16. _____ The Benjamites took wives from **(a)** Jerusalem; **(b)** Jabesh-Gilead; **(c)** Shiloh.

17. _____ The high priest at this time was the **(a)** son; **(b)** grandson; **(c)** nephew of Aaron.

FOR RESEARCH:

18. Find in Genesis an incident similar to Judges 19.22–26. Why was this accepted behavior?

19. Find in Num. 31 an incident similar to Judges 21.10–14. Was this sanctioned by God? Does God handle his enemies in the same way today?

FOR DISCUSSION:

20. Find both good and bad examples in these characters.

21. Why was the whole tribe of Benjamin punished? (See Rev. 2.20–22; Rom. 1.28–32).

22. After Benjamin's punishment, how did Israel treat her? How can we apply this today?

WIVES—A SURVEY

GOD'S PURPOSE FOR A WIFE: _____

A. Figurative descriptions:

Gen. 2.18–25	Prov. 21.9; 25.24
Psalm 128.3	Prov 21.19
Prov. 12.4	Prov. 30.21–23
Prov. 18.22	Ezek. 24.15–18
Prov. 19.13	

1. What can we learn about what God expects a wife to be (or not to be) from each of these descriptions?

A. Help _____

B. Fruitful vine _____

C. Crown _____

D. Rottenness in the bones _____

E. A good thing _____

F. A continual dropping _____

G. Worse than dwelling in the corner of a housetop _____

_____

H. Worse than dwelling in a desert _____

I. Cause of earthquakes _____

J. Desire of the eyes _____

B. Relationship to husband

Gen. 2.18,23,24   1 Cor. 11.3,8,9,11,12

Gen. 3.16   Heb. 13.4

1 Cor. 7.4

2. What does it mean to be "meet?" _____

3. In what ways can a wife be meet for her husband?_____

_____

4. Which of our obligations to our parents becomes limited when we marry?

_____

5. Using Gen. 4.7 as an aid, explain the meaning of Gen. 3.16. _____

_____

6. To whom does a person give power over his/her body? _____

_____

7. Who is the head of the woman? _____

Is the woman inferior to man? (Is Christ inferior to God?) _____

_____

8. Can man and woman be independent of each other? _____

_____

C. Duties

Gen. 2.18–25   1 Cor. 7.1–5, 12–16

Gen. 18.1–8   1 Cor. 14.34,35

Num. 30.6–16   Eph. 5.22–24, 33

Prov. 14.1   Col. 3.18

Prov. 19.14   Titus 2.4

Prov. 31.13–27   1 Peter 3.1–6

9. How has a discouraging and nagging wife failed in her duties? _____

_____

10. What is the biggest help a wife can be? _____

11. What domestic duties does a wife have? _____
_____

12. Does a husband have any say in his wife's spiritual obligations? _____

13. In what ways can we "build our house" or "tear it down?" _____
_____

14. Where does a wife go to learn how to be a good wife? _____
_____

15. What physical obligations does a wife have to her husband? _____
_____

16. What obligations does a wife have in teaching her husband? _____
_____

17. What command is given to wives of prophets? _____

18. Is their any limit to obedience to husbands? _____

19. How should we "fear" our husbands? _____
_____

20. What feelings should we have about our husbands? _____

21. How do we go about calling our husbands "lord" (sir)? _____
_____

FOR DISCUSSION:

22. What are some good and poor reasons for marrying?

23. Did God intend for everyone to marry?

24. In the light of Luke 14.20, how may a wife fail her husband in regard to his spiritual duties?

VII. MOTHERS AND DAUGHTERS

Mothers and daughters have special obligations to each other. The following women give us examples primarily in that area. As we have studied in the past, a mother is a steward to God of the soul he has given her—a child. She is to care for this child so as to give it back to Him in the condition He would have it be. And that child—though a loving mother would never act as if her child owed her anything (Luke 6.32–35)—has certain responsibilities to her parents both as she is raised and when she becomes an adult. This section is the example of the principles God has set forth in Eph. 6.1–4.

LOT'S WIFE AND DAUGHTERS

Text: *Gen. 11.27–32; 13.1–13; 14.1–16; 18.16–33; 19; Luke 17.22–37;*
2 Peter 2.4–9

EXAMPLE: _____

PURPOSE: _____

SHORT ANSWER:

1. How were Abraham and Lot related? _____

2. What did Abraham and Lot do together? _____
_____

3. What caused trouble between them? _____

4. What choice did Lot make? _____

5. Where did this choice eventually lead him? _____

6. From whom did Abraham rescue him? _____

7. Where do we have first mention of Lot's wife? _____
_____

8. Why did Abraham bargain with God to save Sodom? _____
_____

9. For how many righteous would God save Sodom? _____

10. When the two angels came, why did Lot "urge them greatly" not to sleep in the streets? _____

11. What compromise did he make with the Sodomites? _____
_____

12. Altogether, how many daughters did Lot have? _____

13. How many people escaped Sodom? _____

14. How far did Lot's wife go before looking back? _____

15. How did Lot and his daughters choose a refuge? _____
_____

16. Why did Lot's daughters conspire to seduce him? _____
_____

17. What nations sprang from these unions? _____

FOR DISCUSSION:

18. In what ways were Noah and Lot and the circumstances they found themselves in alike?

19. What evidence do we have of Lot's faulty judgment? What personality traits caused this? Reconcile with 2 Peter 2.7.

20. How did Lot's relationship with Abraham save him?

21. What principle of God's judgment can we learn from Gen. 18.23–32, Mt. 5.13; and 2 Peter 2.4–9? Besides the destruction of Sodom, when else has God demonstrated this principle?

22. Why should we "remember Lot's wife?"

23. Contrast Lot's wife and Sarah in their subjection to their husbands.

24. How does Lot's choice of land compare with his daughters' choice of husbands?

25. Should choosing where we live be in any way based on spiritual matters, or on social and economic matters only?

26. Why do you think Lot's daughters were so immoral?

JOCHEBED, PHAROAH'S DAUGHTER, AND ZIPPORAH

Text: Ex. 1.15,16; 2; 4.10–26; 18; Gen. 17.9–14; 25.1,2; Num. 26.59; Acts 7.20–29; Heb. 11.23–26

EXAMPLE: _____

PURPOSE: _____

MATCHING:

1. ____ Moses' mother	**A.** Miriam
2. ____ Moses' father-in-law	**B.** Pharoah's daughter
3. ____ Jochebed's husband	**C.** Zipporah
4. ____ Jochebed's tribe	**D.** Reuel
5. ____ Midian's father	**E.** Jochebed
6. ____ Moses' sister	**F.** Keturah
7. ____ Moses' foster mother	**G.** Jethro
8. ____ Moses' wife	**H.** Levi
9. ____ Zipporah's ancestress	**I.** Amram
10. ____ Jethro	**J.** Abraham

SHORT ANSWER:

11. How did Jochebed manifest her faith? _____

12. How and by whom was Moses discovered? _____
_____

13. How was Jochebed's faith in God vindicated? _____

14. How did Pharoah's daughter treat Moses? _____

15. How did Moses meet his wife? _____

16. What reason did Moses give Jethro for returning to Egypt? _____
_____

17. Why did God seek to kill Moses? _____

18. Who saved him and how? _____

19. Why did Zipporah call Moses a "bridegroom of blood?" _____
_____

20. Did Zipporah go to Egypt with Moses? _____

21. Why did Amram and Jochebed try to save Moses?
22. How was Pharoah's daughter different from her father?
23. What contribution did Jethro make to Jewish law?
24. How did each of these women contribute to Moses' life?
25. Compare Jochebed and Pharoah's daughter as mothers to Moses.

FOR RESEARCH:

26. Find information concerning the Cushite woman in Num. 12.1.

JOB'S WIFE AND DAUGHTERS
Text: *Job 1,2; 42.10–17*

EXAMPLE: _____

PURPOSE: _____

SHORT ANSWER:

1. What was the reason Satan gave for Job's faith in God? _____
_____

2. What did God give Satan permission to do? _____
_____

3. When Satan failed the first time, what reason did he give? _____

4. What limit did God set upon Satan then? _____

5. What did his wife say to him? _____

LISTING:

6. The things Job lost: _____
_____

7. What God gave him "in the latter end:" _____
_____

FOR DISCUSSION:

8. Why did Satan take things from Job? What can we infer, then, from the fact that he took his daughters and left his wife?

9. How did Job answer his wife? In what ways was she foolish?

10. What should Job's wife have said or done for him in his distress?

11. In what ways do we sometimes discourage our husbands?

12. How can daughters be a blessing to their fathers (and mothers) as Job's daughters evidently were?

TWO MOTHERS

Text: 1 Kings 3.5–28

EXAMPLE: _____

PURPOSE: _____

TRUE OR FALSE:

1. T F God came to Solomon in a dream.

2. T F God had promised David a son on the throne.

3. T F Solomon was a child when he became king.

4. T F Solomon had a lot of experience at being king.

5. T F Israel was a large nation.

6. T F God gave only the wisdom requested to Solomon.

7. T F Solomon had to meet no conditions to keep what God gave him.

8. T F The two women lived in the same house.

9. T F The two women had their sons on the same day.

10. T F The women had witnesses to back up their stories.

SHORT ANSWER:

11. How did the one baby die? _____

12. How did the unsuspecting woman find out the baby she had was dead? _____
_____

13. What did Solomon propose to do? _____
_____

14. What was the logic behind Solomon's solution?

15. What was commendable about the real mother?

16. Could Solomon have handled this situation if God had not given him wisdom?

17. What can we learn about the kind of love we should have for our children?

18. At what times in her children's lives does a mother's true love demand that she "give up" some of that child?

RIZPAH

Text: 2 Sam. 21.1–14; Josh. 9.3–21; Ex. 34.11–16; Deut. 7.1,2; 21.22–23

EXAMPLE: _____

PURPOSE: _____

SHORT ANSWER:

1. Who sinned and caused the famine? _____

2. For what did the Gibeonites ask? _____

3. Whom did David spare? _____

Whom were taken? _____

4. When were they put to death? _____

5. What did Rizpah do? _____

6. When David heard what did he do? _____

_____

FOR DISCUSSION:

7. Why did Rizpah do what she did?

8. What examples does she set as a mother?

9. What examples does she set as a woman of God's people seeking to get a wrong righted?

FOR RESEARCH:

10. How had the Gibeonites gotten the original Israelites to make an oath not to slay them? Compare this with Paul's warning in 2 Cor. 11.3 and Gal. 1.8,9.

11. How do we know that the name "Michal" in 21.8 is a scribal error and should be "Merab" instead?

MOTHERS (AND FATHERS)—A SURVEY

GOD'S PURPOSE FOR PARENTS: _____

I.	Duty to Teach	Influence of Parents on Children
	Ex. 10.2	Gen. 6.5–8, 18
	Ex. 12.26,27	Psalm 103.17
	Deut. 4.9,10	1 Kings 22.42,43,51–53
	Deut. 6.4–9, 20–24	2 Kings 15.1–3,32–34
	Deut. 32.46	Ex. 20.4,5
	Psalm 78.5	Jer. 9.13–16
	Prov. 22.6	Ezek. 16.44,45
	Isa. 38.19	2 Kings 8.16–18, 25–27
	Joel 1.3	1 Kings 15.25,26
	Eph. 6.4	2 Chron. 22.3–5

1. How are we commanded to bring up our children? _____
_____

2. In order to do this, what things must we teach them? _____
_____

3. What helps did God give us in this task? _____
_____

4. What must we ourselves do before we can ever hope to teach our children?
_____

5. How does God stress the importance of this duty? _____
_____

6. Is this duty a suggestion or a law? _____

7. If we fail with our children, what will happen to their children? _____
_____

8. How do our lives effect our children? _____

9. If we see something wrong in our children, what indications might there be
about our own lives? _____

10. Share some practical suggestions about how to teach children. _____

II. Duty to Discipline

Gen. 18.19	Prov. 23.13,14
Prov. 3.12	Prov. 29.15,17
Prov. 13.24	1 Thes. 2.11
Prov. 19.18	1 Tim. 3.4,5,12
Prov. 22.15	

11. What is one way God has of judging a man's character? _____
_____

12. What does discipline show about a parent's feeling for a child? _____
_____

13. From what do we save our children when we discipline them? _____
_____

14. Is physical punishment ordained of God? _____
Is there any limit placed on it? _____

15. Do we get any benefits from disciplining our children? _____
_____

16. What things should go along with punishment and rebuke to make them effective? _____

III. Other Duties

Prov. 13.22	Col. 3.21
Prov. 31.21,26,27	1 Tim. 5.8
Isa. 66.13	Titus 2.4
2 Cor. 12.14	

17. What duties do we have in regard to our children's physical well-being? _____
_____

18. What about their emotional well-being? _____

19. Contrast Isa. 49.15 with Titus 2.4. What part of "loving our children" must be learned? _____

IV. Showing Love for Our Children

For each verse or group of verses given, what deed shows love?

20. Ex. 2.1–3; Gen. 33.1,2; 1 Kings 3.23–27 _____

21. 1 Sam. 2.19 _____

22. 2 Sam. 12.15–23; Mark 5.23 _____

23. 2 Sam. 21.8–10 _____

24. Luke 2.48 _____

25. 1 Chron. 22.6–16 _____

26. 2 Tim. 1.5 _____

27. Psalm 103.13 _____

28. Prov. 23.13,14 _____

29. Luke 11.11–13 _____

V. How did the parents in the following two cases do *something wrong in the name of love?*

30. 1 Sam. 2.27–36; 3.13,14 _____

31. 1 Kings 1.6,7 _____

DAUGHTERS (AND SONS)—A SURVEY

GOD'S PURPOSE FOR CHILDREN: _____

I. Duty to Parents

Honor:	Ex. 20.12	Obey:	Deut. 21.18–21
	Lev. 19.3,32		Prov. 30.17
	Deut. 5.16		Rom. 1.28–32
	Job 32.6,7		Eph. 6.1
	Prov. 23.22		Col. 3.20
	Eph. 6.2,3		2 Tim 3.1–5
Care for:	Mt. 15.3–9	Good	Ex. 21.15,17
	Mark 7.8–13	behavior:	Lev. 20.9
	1 Tim. 5.8,16		Prov. 10.1

1. In what ways can we honor our parents? _____

_____

2. What promise do we have if we do this? _____

3. Are little children accountable for sin? _____

Then whom do these passages apply to? _____

4. With what sins does God classify disobedience to parents? _____

5. What limitation is placed on obedience to parents? _____

_____

6. What things are we commanded not to do to our parents? _____
_____

7. What excuse do some people give for not taking care of their parents? _____
_____

8. Why should we be especially careful to take care of our parents who are Christians? _____

II. Duty to God

Psalm 119.9	Jer. 3.25
Psalm 148.12,13	1 Tim. 4.12
Prov. 28.7	2 Tim. 2.22
Eccl. 11.9–12.8 w/ Gen. 8.21	

9. What has God given young people to help them? _____
_____
_____
_____

10. What should be a young person's attitude toward God? _____
_____

11. Is there any special profit in youth? _____

12. What is the fallacy of the "sowing wild oats" philosophy? _____
_____

13. How might men "despise thy youth?" _____

14. What special care should a young person take in this matter? _____
_____

15. If a person still persists in despising youth, what judgment can we make about him? _____

16. In turning away from youthful lusts what do we turn to? _____
_____

17. What are youthful lusts? _____

III. Duty to Learn

Prov. 1.8,9	Prov. 6.20–25	Prov. 15.5,20
Prov. 3.1–3	Prov. 8.32,33	Eccl. 4.13
Prov. 5.1,2	Prov. 13.1	2 Tim. 3.15

18. Does the Bible demand that the children pay attention to their parents' instruction? _____

19. Why are they wiser than their children? _____

20. In what ways will their instruction and advice help? _____

_____

21. What does the Bible call a young person who does not like to be told what to do or who gets angry when corrected? _____

_____

22. What does the Bible say about a young person who knows how to receive instruction and correction properly? _____

23. When should one start to learn about God? _____

IV. Good Examples
For each verse or group of verses tell what the child/children did that should or should not be imitated by young people today.

24. Gen. 9.23 _____

25. Gen. 22.6–12 _____

26. Gen. 44.18–34 _____

27. Gen. 47.11,12; Ruth 2.1,2,17,18 _____

28. Gen. 50.1–13 _____

29. 1 Sam. 2.26; Luke 2.52 _____

30. 1 Sam. 9.5 _____

31. 1 Kings 2.19,20 _____

32. 2 Chron. 34.1–3 _____

33. 2 Tim. 1.5; 3.15 _____

V. Bad Examples

34. Gen. 9.20,22 _____

35. Gen. 19.14; 21.9; 2 Kings 2.22–23 _____

36. 1 Sam. 2.12, 22–25 _____

37. 1 Sam. 8.3 _____

38. 2 Sam. 15 _____

39. 1 Kings 22.51,52 _____

VIII. THE WOMEN IN JESUS' MINISTRY

Several women mentioned in the Gospels were important to Jesus' ministry. We have already discussed many of them who helped and supported Him. However, many women came to Jesus in need, and by answering their need He was able to teach the world a little more about Himself and His kingdom, the church.

PETER'S WIFE AND MOTHER-IN-LAW

Text: Mt. 8.14–17; Mark 1.29–31; Luke 4.38,39; 1 Cor. 9.1–14; 7.39; 1 Tim. 3.11; 1 Peter 3.5,6; 1 Peter 5.1

EXAMPLE: _____

PURPOSE: _____

TRUE OR FALSE:

1. T F Peter's mother-in-law had an unclean spirit.

2. T F She was living in Andrew's house.

3. T F The apostles were with Jesus when he healed her.

4. T F As soon as she was able she took care of Jesus.

5. T F Peter's wife was not a Christian.

6. T F Paul said he had a right to marry a Christian.

7. T F Peter's wife went with him when he preached.

FOR DISCUSSION:

8. How does Jesus "bear our infirmities" today? (See original quote: Isa. 53.4–6)

9. How can we minister to Jesus today?

10. Considering 1 Pet. 5.1 what do we know about the character of Peter's wife?

11. In what ways did Peter's wife follow Sarah's example?

12. Does Scripture command anyone to marry or be married to a Christian? Whom did Paul say he had a right to marry? What is the safest course for all Christians?

13. What is Paul attempting to prove in listing his rights as an apostle?

FOR RESEARCH:

14. What do our Catholic friend teach concerning the woman in 1 Cor. 9.5? Why?

JAIRUS' DAUGHTER AND THE WOMAN WITH AN ISSUE OF BLOOD

Text: Mt. 9.18–26; Mark 5.21–43; Luke 8.41–56

EXAMPLE: _____

PURPOSE: _____

MULTIPLE CHOICE (COMPARE ALL THREE ACCOUNTS):

1. _____ When Jairus came to Jesus, his daughter **(a)** was already dead; **(b)** was headed for inevitable death; **(c)** had been dead four days; **(d)** was not near death.

2. _____ The woman's disease **(a)** was not terminal; **(b)** was arrested though not cured; **(c)** was worse; **(d)** was somewhat better though not cured.

3. _____ The woman touched Jesus' garment **(a)** so she would be healed; **(b)** to get his attention; **(c)** so she could tell others she had touched him; **(d)** so she could worship him.

4. _____ Jesus knew she had touched him because **(a)** he was all-knowing; **(b)** he saw her do it; **(c)** felt her touch; **(d)** he felt the healing power leave him.

5. _____ The woman was healed when **(a)** she touched him; **(b)** He said, "Thy faith hath made thee whole"; **(c)** Jesus asked who touched him; **(d)** she confessed that she had touched him.

6. _____ The woman was healed because **(a)** she touched his clothes; **(b)** she confessed she had touched him; **(c)** Jesus said she was; **(d)** she had faith that if she just toughed his garment she would be healed.

7. _____ Jesus took **(a)** 3; **(b)** 4; **(c)** 5; **(d)** 6 people into Jairus' house.

8. _____ The people laughed at Jesus because **(a)** he said the girl was asleep; **(b)** he said he could raise her from the dead; **(c)** he asked why they were crying; **(d)** he wouldn't let anyone into the house.

9. _____ When Jesus said she was asleep he meant **(a)** she was asleep; **(b)** she was in a coma; **(c)** she was dead and gone; **(d)** she was dead but he could raise her.

FOR DISCUSSION:

10. What was the disease the woman had? Why might she have approached him from behind?

11. What lesson does the woman teach us?

12. What can we say about Jairus' attitude:
    A. When he first came to Jesus;
    B. While the woman was being healed;
    C. When he received word that his daughter was dead;
    D. When everyone laughed at Jesus.

13. How does the raising of Jairus' daughter dispute modern faith healing practices?

THE SINFUL WOMAN

Text: Luke 7.36–50

EXAMPLE: _____

PURPOSE: _____

SHORT ANSWER:

1. Who invited Jesus to dinner? _____
2. Who discovered Jesus' whereabouts? _____
3. What did she do? _____
4. What did Simon think about this? _____
5. What parable did Jesus tell? _____
   _____
6. According to this parable, what caused this woman to love Jesus so much?
   _____

FOR RESEARCH:

7. How do we know this is a different incident than that recorded in Mt. 26, Mark 14, and John 12?

FOR DISCUSSION:

8. How does Jesus contrast Simon with this woman?
9. How did her faith save her?
10. What can the contrast of these two Jews—God's people—teach Christians—God's people today?

THE SYROPHENOECIAN WOMAN

Text: Mt. 15.21–28; Mark 7.24–30

EXAMPLE: _____

PURPOSE: _____

SHORT ANSWER:

1. Where did Jesus go? Why? _____
2. Why did the woman come to Jesus? _____
3. With what complaint did the disciples come to Jesus? _____
   _____

4. How did the woman show her great faith? _____

5. How did Jesus reward her great faith? _____

FOR RESEARCH:

6. What reputation do Tyre and Sidon have in the scriptures?

7. Find out more about this woman's nationality.

FOR DISCUSSION:

8. Explain the analogy of the dogs and the children.

9. How does Jesus' action in this incident foreshadow the gospel?

10. What does this miracle show about the power of Jesus?

11. How is this woman an example to all mothers?

THE WOMAN TAKEN IN ADULTERY
Text: John 7.53–8.11

EXAMPLE: _____

PURPOSE: _____

SHORT ANSWER:

1. What was Jesus doing when the scribes and Pharisees brought the woman?
   _____

2. What question did they ask him? _____

3. How did Jesus turn the question towards them? _____
   _____

4. What did they do? _____

5. What did Jesus tell the woman? _____

TRUE OR FALSE:

6. T F Jesus condoned adultery.

7. T F Jesus broke the Law of Moses by not demanding stoning.

FOR RESEARCH:

8. Whom do some commentators say this woman was?

9. What evidence did Jesus have that this was a trap?

10. How does Jesus combine compassion with exhortation? What does this teach us?

11. How is Jesus' general attitude toward women a better way than the law of Moses?

THE WOMAN WHO WAS BOWED TOGETHER
Text: Luke 13.10–17

EXAMPLE: _____

PURPOSE: _____

SHORT ANSWER:

1. What was Jesus doing on the Sabbath? _____

2. Whom did he see? _____

3. What did he do for her? _____

4. How did the ruler react? _____

5. How did Jesus silence him? _____

6. What did the multitudes do? Why? _____

FOR DISCUSSION:

7. Why did the ruler react as he did? At what other times was Jesus chastised for this same reason?

8. How was this woman "bound by Satan?" Was it sin which caused her deformity?

9. Whom did Jesus say were Abraham's children? (John 8.31–45) In what way was this woman a "daughter of Abraham?"

10. How can we as Gentiles be considered "daughters of Sarah"? (1 Peter 3.6)

IX. THE WORTHY WOMAN

Text: *Prov. 31.10–31*

1. For each verse, write one word that will describe that trait of the worthy woman, e.g., trustworthy, diligent, etc.

2. Beside each word list something comparable to what this woman did that we can do today to exemplify that trait, and something we can require of our daughters to prepare them to be this kind of woman.

3. From all these women we have studied find one who best fits each quality listed and/or who shows the opposite.

4. From all the study we have done in the various sections, list several things we can do to further God's plan for the redemption of mankind.

COMPREHENSIVE REVIEW: WOMEN OF GENESIS

Leah	Rachel	Tamar
Rebekah	Hagar	Bilhah
Sarah	Eve	Zilpah
Dinah	Shua's daughter	

WHO DID IT?

1. Lied to a Pharoah
2. Lied to Abimelech
3. Fed three angels
4. Disguised herself
5. Gave water to a man and camels
6. Used mandrakes
7. At first barren
8. Was "kidnapped"
9. Had her name changed
10. Gave her handmaid to her husband

WHICH WOMAN GAVE US THE EXAMPLE…?

11. Not to be partial to our children
12. Not to be jealous
13. Not to be in subjection to our husbands
14. Not to be deceived by craftiness
15. Not to be modest instinctively
16. To take care for our bodies
17. To obey the laws of God
18. Not to venture where we do not belong
19. Not to deceive our husbands
20. To have faith
21. Not to steal

WHO WERE THEIR WIVES?

22. Jacob
23. Adam
24. Judah
25. Abraham
26. Isaac

WHO WERE THEIR MOTHERS?

27. Seth
28. Isaac
29. Cain
30. Ishmael
31. Esau
32. Perez
33. Judah
34. Benjamin
35. Jacob
36. Onan

WHICH HEIR DID GOD CHOOSE?

37. Cain or Seth
38. Ham, Shem, or Japheth
39. Eleazer, Ishmael, Midian, or Isaac
40. Jacob or Esau
41. Reuben, Judah, Joseph, or Levi
42. Perez, Er, or Onan

THE PROMISES

43. What are the three parts to the promise to Abraham?
44. By what or whom were they fulfilled?
45. We have studied the seed promise as given to what five people?

COMPREHENSIVE REVIEW: WOMEN WHO WERE LEADERS

Queens	False prophetesses	Spiritists
Exorcists	Judges	Prophetesses
Witches	Astrologers	Satanists
Wise women		

WHICH GROUP FULFILLED THESE PURPOSES FOR GOD?

1. Speak commands for God
2. Deliver Israel from the despoilers
3. Execute vengeance of God upon the evil-doer (criminal)
4. Foretell future events
5. Arbitrate and give advice

WHICH GROUP IS DESCRIBED BY EACH STATEMENT?

6. One who seeks to cast out demons.
7. One who believes in the existence of a present and active spirit world and engages in seances as a part of worship.
8. One who foretells the future by the position of the heavenly bodies.
9. One who worships Satan.
10. One who has a familiar spirit and practices sorcery.
11. One who says she speaks from God but does not.

Miriam	Anna	Jezebel the prophetess
Huldah	Philip's daughters	Jehosheba
Deborah	Phineas' wife	Wise woman of Abel
Noadiah	Witch of Endor	Manasseh
Jael	Widow with two mites	Woman of Tekoa
Athaliah	Widow whose sons were	Widow of Nain
Isaiah's wife	nearly sold	

WHICH WOMAN IS BEING DESCRIBED?

12. Hammered a tent pin into Sisera's head
13. Virgins who prophesied
14. Was a widow seven years from her virginity
15. Taught fornication and eating things sacrificed to idols in the early church
16. Had a son whom Jesus raised from the dead
17. Because of a miracle performed by Elisha, she sold enough oil to pay her creditors

18. Was a man, not a woman
19. Gave all that she had
20. Prophesied the fate of Judah to king Josiah
21. Queen of Judah
22. Told David a story
23. Brought forth (by God's power—not her own) the ghost of Samuel
24. Bore a son who was a symbol in a prophecy
25. Plotted to cause Nehemiah to sin
26. Aaron's sister
27. Stole her nephew from the royal nursery
28. Killed all but one of her grandchildren
29. Persuaded Joab not to kill innocent people in a chase for one man
30. A member of the church at Thyatira
31. Miraculously stricken with and cured of leprosy
32. Prophesied concerning Jesus when he was an infant
33. Led Barak and Israel in a battle against the Canaanites
34. Wicked offspring of Ahab and Jezebel
35. Moses' sister
36. Married a priest
37. Whose father was one of the seven at the church in Jerusalem
38. Died in childbirth
39. Helped lead the Israelites out of Egypt
40. Led Judah into national witchcraft, but later repented
41. A poetess

ANSWER IN A FEW WORDS

42. How does God limit women as leaders in the church?
43. How does God limit women as leaders in the world?
44. Does God place any limits on the man?

COMPREHENSIVE REVIEW: MINISTERS AND STEWARDS

Mary of Bethany
Martha
Manoah's wife
Widow of Zarephath
Mary of Rome
Susannah
Elisabeth

Lois
Dorcas
Hannah
Mary of Jerusalem
Joanna
Lydia
Shunemite woman

Mary, wife of Cleopas
Priscilla
Mary, Christ's mother
Salome
Eunice
Mary Magdalene
Peninnah

WHICH WOMAN IS BEING DESCRIBED?

1. Mother of at least one apostle
2. The church at Jerusalem met in her home
3. A tentmaker
4. Fed Elijah
5. Complained to Jesus about her sister
6. Made clothes for poor saints
7. Made a coat for her son every year
8. Anointed Jesus' feet
9. Wife of Chuzas, Herod's steward
10. Helped teach Apollos
11. From whom seven demons were cast out
12. Barren at first
13. Lazarus' sister
14. Had unfeigned faith
15. Housed Paul
16. Built a room for Elisha
17. Asked special places in the kingdom for her sons
18. A seller of purple
19. Raised from the dead
20. Has a child who was raised from the dead
21. Devoted her son to Jehovah from the time he was weaned
22. Married a Greek
23. Left her home during a famine at the word of Elisha
24. Two wives of the same man
25. Temporarily followed the Nazirite vow
26. Bestowed much labor on a church
27. Ministered to Jesus
28. Experienced miraculous childbirth

WHO ARE THEIR MOTHERS?

29. John Mark
30. Timothy
31. Emmanuel
32. Samson
33. John the Baptist
34. Samuel
35. Eunice
36. James and John
37. James and Jesus

WHAT WOULD YOU BE IF YOU DID THIS? (MINISTER OR STEWARD)

38. Fed and housed a preacher
39. Raised a child in the nurture and admonition of the Lord
40. Made clothes for the poor
41. Used our spare time and energy to preach
42. Let a church meet in our home
43. Cleaned the meetinghouse
44. Pray for and encourage each other
45. Correct someone in error

COMPREHENSICE REVIEW: YOUNG WOMEN

Mahlah	Esther	Hoglah
Jephthah's daughter	Tamar	Shulamite shepherdess
Noah	Naaman's servant	Tircah
Milcah	Rhoda	

WHO IS BEING DESCRIBED?

1. The daughters of Zelophehad
2. A judge's daughter
3. A king's daughter
4. Queen of Persia
5. Refused to marry Solomon
6. Never married
7. Told about Elisha
8. Had a good suntan
9. Carried away captive

WHO ACCOMPLISHED EACH PURPOSE?

10. Saved the Jewish race from annihilation
11. Helped change the inheritance laws
12. Fulfilled her father's vow
13. Taught us about true love
14. Unwittingly instrumental in the selection of a son of David to carry the genealogy

RELATIONSHIPS:

15. Descendant of Joseph through Manasseh
16. First cousin to Mordecai
17. David's daughter
18. Maid to John Mark's mother
19. Married her first cousin
20. Same as Hadassah
21. An only child
22. An orphan

OBLIGATIONS:

23. How does God show the importance he places on keeping oneself pure?
24. What may the unmarried do to further God's plan?

COMPREHENSIVE REVIEW: GENTILE WOMEN

Hagar
Rahab
Ruth
Potiphar's wife
Queen of Sheba

Herodias
Woman of Timnah
Bernice
Jezebel
Orpah

Samaritan woman
Drusilla
Delilah
Naomi
Herodias' daughter

WHOSE NATION?

1. Egypt
2. Philistia
3. Idumea
4. Sidon
5. Moab
6. Canaan
7. Israel
8. Some say Ethiopia

WHO IS BEING DESCRIBED?

9. A harlot
10. Naomi's daughter-in-law
11. Queen of the south
12. Sarah's handmaid
13. Danced for Herod
14. Felix's wife
15. Agrippa's sister
16. Philip's wife
17. Samson's wife
18. Joseph's temptress
19. David's great-grandmother
20. Ahab's wife
21. Boaz's wife
22. Boaz's mother
23. Samson's mistress
24. Naboth's murderess
25. Had five husbands
26. Mara

27. Descendant of Esau
28. Descendant of Lot

WHOSE PURPOSE?

29. An example to go to any lengths to seek our salvation
30. To get Joseph into a place of authority
31. To bear children in the line of Christ
32. To give God an occasion against the Philistines
33. To teach others about Christ
34. To send Paul to Rome
35. To help Israel take the promised land
36. To show that God always keeps his promises
37. To show the reason for the rejection of the northern ten tribes
38. To demonstrate the wrong attitude to take toward the truth
39. To demonstrate that God's authority is above all others
40. Not revealed
41. To show the position of the Jews and the Law of Moses
42. To decrease John, so that Jesus could increase

COMPREHENSIVE REVIEW: WIVES

Abigail
Michal
Haggith
Jeroboam's wife

Solomon's wives
Bathsheba
Levite's concubine
Sapphira

Gomer
Pharoah's daughter
Abishag
Merab

WHO WERE THEIR WIVES?

1. David
2. Solomon
3. Nabal
4. Ananias
5. Hosea
6. Uriah
7. Paltiel

WHO WERE THEIR MOTHERS?

8. Jezreel
9. Solomon
10. Loruhammah
11. Adonijah
12. Jedidiah
13. Loammi

WHO IS BEING DESCRIBED?

14. Went to Ahijah
15. Took food to David
16. Lied to the Holy Spirit
17. Put idols in a bed
18. Bathed in an open place
19. Went home to daddy
20. Was an idolater
21. Nursed David
22. Corrected her husband disrespectfully
23. Committed adultery
24. Gave good advice
25. Symbolic of Israel
26. Tempted a man to sin
27. Fell down dead
28. Tried to keep her identity a secret
29. Had a sick child
30. Promised to one and given to another
31. Was pretty
32. Was murdered
33. Was bought back
34. A house was built for her
35. Saul's daughter

LISTING

36. Three scriptural figurative descriptions of a good wife.
37. Two descriptions of a poor wife.
38. Five duties we have as a wife.

COMPREHENSIVE REVIEW: MOTHERS AND DAUGHTERS

Lot's wife
Lot's daughters
Job's wife

Job's daughters
Pharoah's daughter
Zipporah

Jochebed
Rizpah
Two mothers

WHO IS BEING DESCRIBED?

1. Hid her child
2. Prettiest girls in the land
3. Looked back
4. Daughter of a priest
5. Harlots
6. Saul's concubine
7. Seduced their father
8. Jemimah, Keziah, and Kerenhappuch
9. Moses' wife
10. Moses' mother
11. Told husband to curse God
12. Cared for her sons' bodies
13. Judged by Solomon
14. Mothers of Moab and Ammon
15. Saved Moses' life

EXAMPLES

16. Showed the sacrificial love a mother should have
17. Set a poor example for her daughters
18. Had faith
19. A pleasure to their father
20. Used as an example for those who would escape the destruction of Jerusalem
21. Kept the law when others had forgotten

DUTIES

22. List some of the duties a mother has to her children
23. List some of the duties a daughter has to her parents

OTHERS

24. Name two other mothers we have studied and the examples they set as mothers
25. Name two other daughters we have studied and the examples they set as daughters

COMPREHENSIVE REVIEW:
THE WOMEN IN JESUS' MINISTRY

The woman with an issue of blood
The woman who was bowed together
The woman taken in adultery
The Syrophoenician woman

The sinful woman
Peter's wife
Peter's mother-in-law
Jairus' daughter

WHO IS BEING DESCRIBED?

1. Had a sick child
2. Lived with an apostle
3. Anointed Jesus' feet
4. Raised from the dead
5. A Gentile
6. Healed by Jesus
7. Ministered to Jesus
8. Forgiven of her sins
9. Had an affliction for 18 years
10. Had an affliction for 12 years
11. Had great faith
12. Had great love
13. Daughter of a Jewish ruler
14. Did not have faith before Jesus
    performed the miracle

**FROM THESE WOMEN WHAT HAVE
WE LEARNED:**

15. About the power of Jesus?
16. About the gospel?
17. About our love for God?
18. About Jesus' authority?
19. About sin?
20. About our spiritual parentage?

Also by Dene Ward

Suitable for Individual or Group Study

Whoso Findeth a Wife

Despite the opinion of today's woman, who believes that being a wife is so simple she must have something real to do with her life, it is not that easy. Too often culture has a way of sneaking into our thinking, and whereas the Scriptures suit all cultures, not all cultures suit the Scriptures. Dene Ward has taken ten metaphors the Bible uses to describe a wife, and, as she always does, shown how those can be used in a practical way to make ourselves into the ideal helper God intended from the beginning. This book can be used as a gift for a new bride, an individual study guide for any wife, or a women's class book with the thought questions included at the end of each essay.

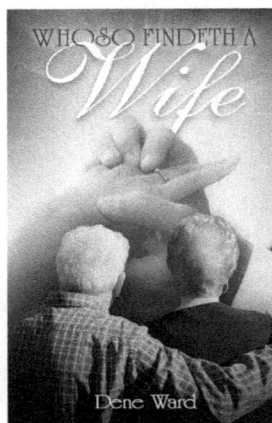

Daily Devotional

Flight Paths

When encroaching blindness took her music teaching career away, Dene Ward turned her attention to writing. What began as e-mail devotions to some friends grew into a list of hundreds of subscribers. Three hundred sixty-six of those devotions have been assembled to form this daily devotional. Follow her through a year of camping, bird-watching, medical procedures, piano lessons, memories, and more as she uses daily life as a springboard to thought-provoking and character-challenging messages of endurance and faith.

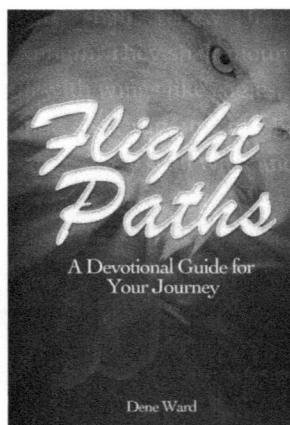

Weekly Devotional

Soul Food

Cooking has always been a part of Dene Ward's life. She grew up in a house where they were always feeding someone and followed that same path as a wife and mother. On the table, she has always offered a nourishing meal; she now offers this collection to feed your souls, lessons from her hearth to your heart.

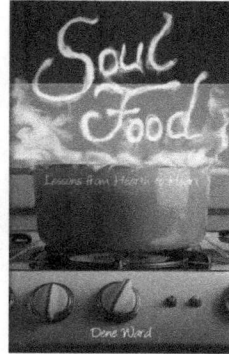

Down a Country Lane

Dene Ward was a city girl who married a country boy. They raised their family in the country, as their father was raised, and she quickly learned about toiling in the garden, chasing loose pigs, looking for snakes in the oddest places, and never taking for granted electricity, running water, and a clear path from the road to the house—half a mile down the country lane. Join her as she shares the lessons she has acquired with hard experience, which have also given her more insight to the rural-based lessons Jesus taught, and find yourself too, a little closer to God.

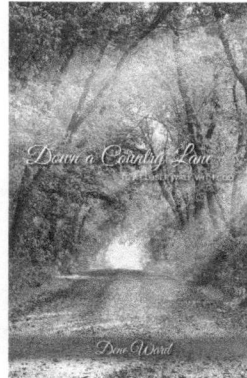

In the Garden with God

Dene Ward and her husband Keith have gardened for nearly 40 years, which has shown her why God's prophets and preachers, including Jesus, used so many references to plants and planting—it's only natural. Join her for a walk in the garden with God.

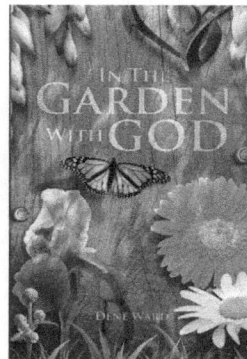

www.ingramcontent.com/pod-product-compliance
Lightning Source LLC
Chambersburg PA
CBHW031628040426
42452CB00007B/727